GENEROUS PEOPLE

EFFECTIVE
CHURCH
SERIES

EUGENE GRIMM

Edited by HERB MILLER

GENEROUS PEOPLE

ABINGDON PRESS
Nashville

GENEROUS PEOPLE

Copyright © 1992 by Abingdon Press

Library of Congress Cataloging-in-Publication Data

Grimm, Eugene, 1945–
  Generous people / Eugene Grimm: edited by Herb Miller.
    p.   cm.—(Effective church series)
  ISBN 0-687-14045-5 (pbk.: alk. paper)
  1. Stewardship, Christian.   2. Christian giving.   I. Miller,
Herb.   II. Title.   III. Series.
BV772.G765   1992
248'.6—dc20   92-18472

MANUFACTURED IN THE UNITED STATES OF AMERICA

CONTENTS

To
my stewardship colleagues in the
Division for Christian Ministries of the
Evangelical Lutheran Church in America

FOREWORD

Research indicates that "cirrhosis of the giver" is increasingly prevalent among American church members. Per-capita giving in all denominations dropped from 3.05 percent of disposable income in 1968 to 2.62 percent in 1989 (with the sharpest decline between 1985 and 1989). Yet many congregations report that their total donations have increased by 15 to 30 percent during the last three years. What causes these statistical opposites?

Leaders in every denomination agree that stewardship is a biblical imperative for all Christians. The word *steward* appears in the Bible twenty-seven times. Jesus said, "From everyone to whom much has been given, much will be required" (Luke 12:48). Church leaders also agree that stewardship is a pragmatic necessity. How else can congregations accomplish their mission of loving God, loving people, and reaching out? Yet how many lay and clergy leaders are highly confident of their ability to help Christians grow in this aspect of their spiritual development?

Eugene Grimm cuts through the clouds of confusion that surround this subject. His down-to-earth prescriptions: (1) move us beyond the myths so prevalent in stewardship; (2) help us learn how to organize, energize, and equip local stewardship leaders; and (3) enable us to see how we can effectively execute stewardship programs in churches of every size.

Each profession contains three kinds of people—those who can write about it, those who can talk about it, and those who can do it. Grimm is one of those exceptional people who has more than two of these skills. He writes well, and as a national staff person for the Evangelical Lutheran Church in America, he is in demand as a speaker and workshop leader. Each year, his on-site leadership helps dozens of congregations achieve 15 to 50 percent increases in their annual stewardship appeals.

Grimm's stewardship insights fit the goal of the Effective Church Series: to help meet the need for "how to" answers in specific areas of church life. Each of these volumes provides clergy and laypeople with practical insights and methods which can increase their congregation's effectiveness in achieving God's purposes in every aspect of ministry: leadership, worship, Sunday school, membership care, biblical literacy, spiritual growth, small groups, evangelism, new-member assimilation, prayer, youth work, singles work, young-adult work, time management, stewardship, administration, community service, world mission, conflict resolution, and writing skills.

Grimm's insights also fit the theological focus of the Effective Church Series. While concentrating more on the practical than on the theoretical and conceptual, its "ideas that work" rest on biblical principles. Without that foundation, method-sharing feeds us a diet of cotton candy—sweet but devoid of nutrients. Grimm has addressed the subject of stewardship in ways consistent with biblical truths and classic Christian theology.

Very few stewardship committees face the problem depicted in the Old Testament book of Exodus, when people gave too much to their church:

> "The people are bringing much more than enough for doing the work that the LORD has commanded us to do." So Moses gave command, and word was proclaimed throughout the camp: "No man or woman is to make anything else as an offering for the sanctuary." So the people were restrained

from bringing; for what they had already brought was more than enough to do all the work. (36:5-7)

Nor do many pastors have people in their churches like the wealthy Texas businessman who co-founded Texas Instruments. (That company's numerous inventions included the first silicone transistor in 1954, the first integrated circuit in 1958, and the first single-chip computer in 1971.) During recent years, this layman has given away 150 million dollars to a variety of worthy causes. He says that his objective is to get it down to the last nickel.

Most church leaders are working with far less spiritually mature people. Stewardship committee chairpeople rarely encounter the difficulty of oversufficiency at church budget preparation time. Seldom do pastors feel the urge to restrain a person like the widow Jesus described, who gave her mite (her very last dollar) to God's work. Evidence from congregations of every denomination indicates, however, that church people can grow significantly in their giving—if someone provides encouragement. Grimm speaks clearly and helpfully to leaders who find themselves in these kinds of "normal" circumstances, and who would prefer to experience the more "abnormal" circumstances of budgetary oversufficiency and sacrificial generosity.

Herb Miller
Lubbock, Texas

INTRODUCTION

Why do some congregations experience higher and higher levels of Christian stewardship each year, while neighboring churches remain in the financial doldrums? This book outlines the spiritual and pragmatic answers to that question.

When I came out of seminary, I was very naive about money. Like many pastors, I never planned to talk much about it. I even believed the myth that many people in congregations resent having the pastor discuss money. Since stewardhip is a result of our spiritual commitment, I also believed that committed Christians would therefore give.

It took only a few short years to shatter most of the illusions.

- People do not "automatically" respond to the gospel with good giving habits.
- Regular church attendance does not translate into strong stewardship levels. People who attend regularly usually give more than the occasional worshipers. But Christians mature at different rates in different directions. A strength in one Christian is often a weakness in another.
- Churches cannot wait until people grow spiritually so they will give; some people cannot grow spiritually until they decide to give. And asking people to improve their treasure management is asking them to grow spirit-

ually—the two matters cannot be separated. When we look at principles for vital stewardship, we are looking at principles that can help people grow spiritually.

Congregations with growing incomes and effective stewardship ministries see stewardship as a vital component in their whole ministry picture. They understand that a systematic and intentional approach to stewardship requires special attention to ten principles. The purpose of this book is to help congregations and stewardship committees focus on those essentials that will bring their ministry of stewardship to new heights of excellence. These principles can also take some of the "stew" out of stewardship— helping stewardship committees learn that stewardship, like other aspects of Christian ministry, can be fun.

Special thanks are due several people, without whom this book could not have been written. Pastor Richard Hollinger, formerly of Saint Paul Lutheran Church in Clearwater, Florida, is a most dynamic stewardship leader. His ministry provided the inspiration for the story in chapter one. Pastor Steve Schick of Archbold, Ohio, provided the letter that opens chapter three. Pastor Glen Clauser of Vandalia, Ohio; Pastor David Hanford of Springfield, Ohio; Pastor Diana Gugal of Adamsville, Ohio; and Ms. Barbara Fullerton of Toronto, Ontario, Canada, provided inspiration and direction for several excellent illustrations.

A word of appreciation also should be given my colleagues in the Division for Congregational Ministries of the Evangelical Lutheran Church in America, to whom this book is dedicated. All of us have served as mentors for one another, and the value I place on their tutelage cannot be expressed in words. A special thanks also to my friend Candy Kerl and my wife Margie, for their help in proofreading and copy editing.

I

FOUNDATIONS FOR OUTWARD-BOUND LIVING

"Wow!" exclaimed a businessman recently appointed to the stewardship committee of a Lutheran church in Florida.

His friend Larry, continuing to sip his coffee, listened as John finished his animated observations.

"At the meeting last night, I saw a list of our church's annual giving totals for the last ten years. How did the pastor get that much money from that number of people? It sure didn't happen in the church we attended where we lived before."

John's friend, a long-time member of the congregation, said, "I'm not sure I can give you a complete answer to that. It's been somewhat of a mystery to all of us. But during the years he has been pastor here, he has built some solid foundations that we live on."

"What kind of foundations?" John asked.

"That's hard to describe," Larry said. "But he is the best I ever saw at taking what the Bible says about money and putting it across to people in commonsense ways. He is always saying that stewardship is more than financial giving; it is the main business of every Christian—stewardship is what we do after we say we believe. When he talks about stewardship, he doesn't stop with money. He says that stewardship relates to every aspect of Christian life. But he sure starts with money. And he has the knack of pulling lots of other people into that way of thinking."

After pausing for another sip of coffee, Larry continued, "Pastor Hollinger takes what he believes about stewardship for individuals and applies it to the whole congregation. We haven't quite reached the goal of giving 50 percent of the church's income to ministries outside the congregation. But we sure are close—$150,000 per year in giving to missions is something to write home about.

"Pastor Hollinger always says that the primary reason we never have financial problems is because we see the call to mission as our prime directive. He must be right. Since I have been here, most of the debates in congregational meetings have centered on how to give away money, rather than how to raise it."

"One sure thing," John said as he cleaned up the crumbs from his fast-food breakfast. "Stewardship is foundational to everything a church does. When the money doesn't fly right, nothing else can get off the ground. The pilots and crews in a lot of churches need to know how to use ideas like his."[1]

John is right. Christian stewardship is basic to all that we do for our Lord. Financial stewardship furnishes the fuel for all our other ministries. The root meaning of the biblical word for *stewardship* is "the management of a household," usually on behalf of someone else. While that management has a financial dimension, it also includes responsibility for everything in the household. A manager cares for, protects, conducts, and administers. Christian stewards are not owners; they are the trustees of an enormous God-given estate. What God gets done through congregations happens through the money that stewards manage.

The Corinthian Foundations

The apostle Paul sets forth an excellent foundation for dynamic Christian stewardship in his letters to the Corinthian church. Writing to a church besieged by controversies and inner conflict, Paul suggests that it first turn its attention outward. He lifts up the needs of the people of Judea, who were suffering from far more serious problems than were the people of Corinth—famine and persecution.

> Now concerning the contribution for the saints: as I directed the churches of Galatia, so you also are to do. On the first day of every week, each of you is to put something aside and store it up, as [you] may prosper, so that contributions need not be made when I come. And when I arrive, I will send those whom you accredit by letter to carry your gift to Jerusalem. If it seems advisable that I should go also, they will accompany me. (1 Cor. 16:1-4 RSV)

Following a seminar presentation led by a prominent psychiatrist, a woman in the back of the room asked a question: "Doctor, what should I do when I feel a nervous breakdown coming on?"

The doctor rubbed his chin and thought for a moment. Then he replied, "When you feel a nervous breakdown coming on, get out of bed, get dressed, leave your house, get into your car, go across town, and do something for somebody." Paul was writing to a church whose members could legitimately have responded, "We've got troubles of our own." Yet like the psychiatrist, Paul says that if we turn our attention toward others, we will see our own difficulties melt like ice cream on a hot, sunny day.

The apostle also presents what may be the most succinct theology for Christian giving and stewardship ever written. In verse two, he makes four admonitions: *First, giving is an act of worship.* On the day of worship, Sunday, set aside an offering. *Second, give systematically.* If we give when we worship, we will give regularly. *Third, give proportionately to income.* We cannot give what we have not received. But we can *withhold* what we have received. Giving an amount in proportion to what we earn—a percentage of our income—controls that selfish human reflex. *Fourth, plan your giving in advance.* "By the time I have arrived," Paul is saying, "the offering will be in hand." These four biblical foundation stones are still as solid as they were twenty centuries ago. They will sustain a strong and effective congregational stewardship education process.

Later, in what many scholars believe was a part of Paul's third Corinthian letter, he introduces us to the example of the people of Macedonia. For the Macedonians, the springs of stewardship that seemed to contain no water overflowed into a large lake of giving. First, their giving was an *example of remarkable generosity:* "Their abundant joy and their extreme poverty have overflowed in a wealth of generosity" (2 Cor. 8:2). Second, their giving was an *example of extreme sacrifice:* "They voluntarily gave according to their means and even beyond their means" (2 Cor. 8:3). Third, their giving was an *example of total involvement:* " . . . begging us earnestly for the privilege of sharing in this ministry to the saints" (2 Cor. 8:4). Fourth, their giving was an *example of a vibrant faith and commitment:* "They gave themselves first to the Lord and, by the will of God, to us" (2 Cor. 8:5). Fifth, their giving was an *example of ultimate trust in God:* "For if the eagerness to give is there, the gift is acceptable according to what one has—not according to what one does not have" (2 Cor. 8:12). There was no pulling in the belts or toeing the budget line here. These people realized that commitment means sacrifice, and they willingly offered what they had for others.

Action Possibility: When confronted with financial hardship or deficits in congregations, remember Paul's advice. Rather than tighten the budget strings and reduce spending, turn your attention outward. While this may not seem to make financial or business sense, it actually does. Businesses

16

do not solve major financial problems by reducing spending, but by increasing income. Churches that focus on reducing spending often tend to increase rather than reduce their financial distress. Budget cuts discourage people from growing. Budget cutbacks are like putting out a press release that says, "We're holding the line so that you can keep giving what you are now giving."

Stewardship Is More Than Money

The experts define Christian stewardship in many ways:
- The believer's response to the creating, redeeming, and sanctifying love of God.
- A way of life that includes the way we manage our whole redeemed lives and our possessions.
- What I do after I say "I believe."
- Caring for all that God has entrusted to us.
- The fruit of saving faith.
- The church in mission.
- The way we use the resources God has entrusted to us for the purposes to which the Lord has called us.

All these are legitimate definitions of Christian stewardship, but each definition involves more than money. Yet, what happens when you ask a group of people, "What is the first thing you think of when I say the word *stewardship?*" The first response is usually, **"MONEY!"** In the minds of many people, stewardship tends to be $teward$hip.

A young minister bemoaned the fact that members of her congregation seemed unable to comprehend the fact that stewardship involves so much more than money. She decided to return to those thrilling days of yesteryear and use a simple program that stressed the three T's—Time, Talent, and Treasure. She broadcast her three-week plan in the church newsletter. The first week she preached a dynamic sermon on the stewardship of time. The second week, she expounded on the importance of using one's talents in ministry. The third week, many people stayed home. They spelled stewardship as $teward$hip.

Dr. Charles Sigel commented that stewardship is something like a bowl of gelatin. No matter how you pick it up, it tends to shake all over. He continued,

> Some people lay hold of stewardship where it touches a person's pocketbook. Then money or financial resources are made its equivalent. That's not all bad, on the one hand, because at least it makes stewardship concrete and tangible enough so that we can sink our teeth into it. . . . But we all recognize that, if we stop with money, we have seriously shortchanged what the Bible intends by stewardship.[2]

In some oriental languages, the word *do* (pronounced *dough*) means "way of." For them, *do* is a system, an entire life-style. Christian stewardship is much like the oriental *do*. It is a life-style. When Christians do stewardship, they do ministry and service.

Stewardship Is Not Less Than Money

A congregation that wants an effective overall ministry realizes that its financial resources are of primary importance. Once the financial stewardship is present, other dimensions of ministry begin to soar.

Two young pastors, one of whom had just started serving his first congregation, and another who was about to be assigned to a student parish, were discussing the first steps one should take upon arriving at a new parish. The more experienced of the two (by several weeks) commented, "The first thing you'll need to do when you get to your church is call a meeting of the finance and stewardship committees." In some ways, the young pastor was wise beyond his years. The foundation of all ministry is the financial stewardship that undergirds it.

Money is as important to the life and mission of a congregation as it is to life itself. Money plays an important role in our whole existence. Society is based on monetary values. We even think in monetary terms when we talk about the value of individuals. Statements like "Joe Williams is worth half a million dollars" suggest that Joe's worth as a person equals his possessions. Christians know that a person's possessions are not what gives that person value in the eyes of God. Yet, we continue to use these slip-of-the-tongue expressions that contradict the truth of the gospel, underscoring how deeply money is rooted in our daily thinking.

Money was just as important in Jesus' day. If we were to strike the comments of Jesus about money, we would reduce his teachings by more than one-third. Sixteen of Jesus' approximately thirty-eight parables dealt with money. One of every seven verses in the first three Gospels in some way deals with money. In fact, Jesus spoke about money more than about any other single subject, except the kingdom of God itself. Perhaps this was because Jesus understood how money itself can become a god. His assertions, "You cannot serve God and wealth" (Matt. 6:24) and, "For where your treasure is, there will your heart be also" (Matt. 6:21) indicate his awareness of the preemptive role played by money in the lives of people.

A new pastor had just arrived on the scene. Members were filing out, greeting him and his family following the first worship service. One member commented, "That was a fine sermon, pastor. I wonder if I might be able to sit down and have a chat with you next week?"

An appointment was made. In the interim, the pastor discovered that the man was one of the patriarchs of the church. During their conversation, the pastor sensed that there was something the man wished to say but was reluctant to express.

The pastor decided to provide an opening: "John, what advice would you give me as a new pastor coming into this congregation? What is it that you, as a long-time member here, know about this church that would be good for me to hear?"

His reluctance gone, John replied, "Pastor, the best word of advice I can give you is to remember that we don't talk about money in this church!"

Among all the stewardship myths thrust upon pastors and church leaders, this is one of the most perverse. Congregations that experience growing incomes and effective ministries *do* talk about money and stewardship. Moreover, they do not reserve that talk only for the time of the congregational campaign or appeal. This mums-the-word-about-money myth, like so many others, is often more easily dispelled than we think. The best way to respond to these malevolent misconceptions is to ask the world's most important question: Why?

Such myths rarely have any sound theological or biblical basis. Many times they are founded on tradition or the fact that a much-loved pastor from years ago did not like to talk about money. In this way, the practice of a single individual can become absolutized for all time—and no one will have the vaguest idea why. Sometimes these notions are based on the mistaken fantasy that all the members of the congregation are doing their best. While it is true that in most congretions there are some who give sacrificially, the vast majority of the people could and would grow, if invited. Experience indicates that on the average, 82 percent of the people who fill out "estimates of giving" cards will increase their giving with the use of an effective stewardship program.

Action Possibility: Conduct a study of the number of households in your congregation that can be counted as "household income equivalents" (HIE). These HIEs provide an effective way to count "giving units" accurately. They equalize couples, single persons, mixed denominational marriages, and people with fixed incomes. With the information gathered, determine the average, or median, income of your congregation, based on the IRS figures for your area. To determine the total income of the congregation, multiply the number of household income equivalents by the average, or median, household income in your community. Check the actual amount members of the congregation gave during the last twelve months. Divide the amount given by members (excluding pass-through giving from event registration fees, etc.) by the total income of all members in the congregation. (See appendix B for forms and further instructions.)

The Three Commandments of Stewardship Ministries

1. Keep it positive.
2. Keep it biblical.
3. Stress the mission.

People do not give to a sinking ship. The "woe is we; we is undone" approach used in many congregations may induce a brief spurt in giving or get a congregation over the immediate hump of unpaid bills. But repeated use of this procedure will boomerang into a repeat of budget difficulties. The long-term result of crying wolf is the need to cry wolf again.

People appreciate knowing that their church teaches the Bible. While proof-texting every request is not a good idea, the members should be aware that their congregation practices biblical stewardship. Try to picture fulfilling the teachings of Jesus in the Sermon on the Mount without financial stewardship. Or think about trying to start a new congregation without a financial foundation. Paul's "invitation" to participate in the offering for the saints of Judea who were in distress compels us to look beyond our own needs and see the plight of others.

The biblical call to stewardship is a call to mission. Appeals that stress the needs of the budget usually fall short. For the leadership of a congregation, the budget may signify the mission that is about to be undertaken. For Mr. and Mrs. Avery Pewsyter, however, the budget is something to vote on once a year. Even program budgets, while vast improvements over the line-item variety, are not looked upon by the average Christian as depicting mission.

Action Possibility: Help the members of your congregation picture in their minds the mission accomplished by your congregation. Consider taking pictures and slides of its various mission activities. Compile these into a taped narration that shares the congregation's Vision for Ministry. Such a vision might include six ministry areas—worship, learning, witness, service, support, and partnership (the ministry your congregation carries out in partnership with other churches, mission fields, or in your denominational mission work). The typical response to seeing all a congregation does is, "WOW! I didn't know we did so much!"

Imagination Generates Energy, Generates Results

It was lunch break at the annual governing board retreat. Members were meeting at the retreat center of a nearby year-round church camp. The setting was rustic and beautiful. After allowing time for the normal chit-chat and catch-up on one another's lives, Barbara called for a few moments of silence.

"What did everyone think of that morning session?" she asked.

Gordon spoke first. "I'm finding myself in something of a state of surprise," he said. "Those exercises our leader had us going through at first seemed to waste a lot of valuable time. But then it all seemed to come together when we started listing our congregation's ministries."

"I enjoyed the exercises," Joan added. "When our leader

said that it would all make sense in a little while, I simply took him at his word. But after we listed everything we do in those six ministries areas, I actually was a little angry with myself."

"Oh? Why?" asked Gordie.

"I should have known about every one of those. Well, I guess maybe I did. But you know, when we were asked to list our ministries in each of the areas he suggested, I just went blank. I could think of only two or three."

"That was my experience, too," commented Abe. "And you know what? I think he knew that we would fall short on that. That's why he was so patient and started asking questions."

"It was a real eye-opener for me, too," interjected Stephanie. "What really struck me was that if we, who are supposed to be the leaders of this congregation, weren't more aware of all our ministries, what about those who are not as active as we are?"

The pastor had been sitting rather quietly, listening as the others spoke. Finally, he entered the conversation.

"You know, folks, it occurs to me that one of the valuable lessons we've learned this morning is that we must do a better job of communicating our mission. How can we expect people to get excited if they don't know what to get excited about?"

"Good point," Barb agreed. "Maybe one of the things we need to do at our next meeting is find better ways to share our mission. I think people would get excited if they heard the story."

Gordie responded, "And I think when people get excited about something, they support it—with both their energy and their dollars. The key to effective support for ministry is unlocking the doors of our imagination. I'd like to serve on a task force to find creative ways to tell our mission story. I still can't get over it. I just didn't know our church did so much! I don't know when I've been more inspired or rarin' to go."

II

TWO VITAL ELEMENTS

Bob's telephone seemed to explode beside his head as he was concentrating on an article for his upcoming stewardship newsletter. He felt a short flash of annoyance as he reached for the phone, then thought to himself, "Oops, attitude adjustment . . . that's why I'm here."

He answered with a cordial, "Stewardship office. This is Bob."

"Hello, Bob, this is Jim Cartwight."

"Jim, it's good to hear from you. How are things going at St. Mark's?"

"Great! I'm calling to tell you it's okay for you to say, 'I told you so.' You said that if we'd follow that appeal we used last fall to the letter, it would work for us. We did, and it did. We netted a 24 percent increase in giving over the previous twelve months. And believe it or not, we've been getting every penny!"

"That's really good to hear, Jim. Are you planning to repeat it this year?" Bob asked.

"Well, that's what I'm calling about. We had a long discussion last night in our governing board meeting. Several members said they could not remember the time when our congregation didn't have some kind of money problems. The fact is, we're actually receiving everything we need to carry out our present program. That prompted a couple of them to ask if perhaps we should skip the stewardship program this year. After all, last year's effort was the only real stewardship appeal they've ever had here. They were a little afraid we might overload our members. In the past, we just sent out a letter asking for commitments. But only about 28 percent of our membership even responded. Last year, 62 percent of our members made estimates.

"I felt a little reluctant, but I told them I'd give you a call today to see what you might suggest. I know what you'll say, but I need ammunition. Some of the board members have gotten the idea that because things are so good right now, we don't have to keep after stewardship. What can I say to them, Bob?"

"First, Jim, I'd suggest that you ask them to recall something I said in that first introductory presentation. Churches with high levels of giving conduct some kind of stewardship appeal *every* year. I believe I also mentioned that every good stewardship campaign stresses the need of the giver to give, rather than the need of the congregation to receive. Not to have a stewardship appeal this year could reinforce the notion that giving to needs is the main reason for giving."

"I remember that. You also said that the congregation needs to do some visioning each year to stretch ourselves and think about what God might have us do that we aren't now doing."

"Right. Our ministry is only as effective as our vision. Virtually every congregation I've ever seen has the potential to expand its ministry."

"Their primary worry was about the expense of a program. Last year our celebration luncheon cost about four dollars per member. They thought that was awfully high."

"Congregations often worry about how much it costs to conduct an effective stewardship appeal. The myth lurking in many congregations whispers that spending money to raise the level of people's consciousness about money is wrong, or even sinful. In truth, an effective stewardship campaign should never be viewed as merely spending money to make money. That would equate Christian stewardship with simple fund-raising.

"There's nothing wrong with fund-raising, of course, but the primary focus of a stewardship campaign should not stop with raising dollars for mission. Fund-raising is a financial matter. Stewardship is primarily a spiritual matter. Fund-raising is concerned with raising money for the budget. Stewardship relates to how we live out our commitment to Jesus Christ.

"We all know that talking about money in some churches has developed a bad reputation. I think the main reason is because those church leaders often focus energy on trying to raise money, rather than on raising the spiritual level of their members. When we spend money to increase stewardship levels, we are actually spending money on the spiritual growth of our members. That is like spending money on Sunday school materials.

"But for those who are stuck in the purely monetary gear, ask them to compare the increase in annual giving they received to the dollars they spent. It's only a fraction. You might also point out—and you can quote me on this one—that the *most expensive* stewardship appeal ever conducted is either the one that fails or the one that wasn't done."

"That's a good one, Bob. I'm writing that down."

"You might also remind them of the other positive benefits of the program. There was a real spirit of celebration after the appeal. The members felt good about their estimates of giving, and more people than ever made estimates."

"Great, I think that when they consider this further, they'll not only agree to have a campaign this fall, but they'll want one. I knew I could count on you for some help. Thanks so much for your thoughts and ideas."

The First Vital Element: An Effective Campaign

What is the key ingredient for increasing the level of stewardship in a congregation? An effective annual stewardship campaign or appeal! A recipe for stewardship that leaves out the annual campaign is like trying to make bread without dough.

An effective campaign does far more than just ask members to increase their giving. While asking is an important ingredient of an appeal, it is only one of four positive benefits.

1. Tell the old old story. Whether it is done through stewardship talks, Sunday school classes for adults and children, the pastor's sermon, the bulletin, or newsletter articles, or a combination of techniques, telling the "old, old story of Jesus and his love" is a mandate for effective stewardship. People need and want to hear the good news of Christ. Scripture texts abound. A stewardship specialist from Minnesota once bought a Bible just for marking the stewardship and money passages. When he finished, it was hard to turn a page anywhere in the New Testament and not find some reference to stewardship or money.

Action Possibility: Consider a stewardship study series during the Sunday school hour. Biblical source material could include: (1) Study the biblical principles of tithes and offerings. (2) The parables of Jesus are a rich fountain of stewardship instruction. Nearly half of them touch on money and the way it affects our Christian lives. (3) Old Testament passages abound with examples of Israel's stewardship . . . and its lack of it.

2. Tell the new new story of mission. Every congregation, small or large, has thirty or more ministries that are a regular part of its mission. They take distinctive forms—sharing audiotapes with homebound members, caring for the poor of the community, leading Bible studies during the week, and other specialized activities. Each of these ministries has a "people" story to tell. People regularly need to hear the story of what their congregation is doing for Christ's sake.

Fact: People give when they are excited about the mission their congregation is doing. The way to generate that excitement is to help them continually marvel at all the congregation is doing. This may also enhance the visioning process of the congregation. Having more members aware of the broadness of the congregation's ministries will encourage new ideas for further mission and increase the level of spiritual commitment.

Action Possibility: Consider holding a mission and ministry planning retreat for your church governing board. First, ask each member to list as many of the ministries of the congregation as possible. Then systematically list all the things your congregation is doing in the ministry areas of *worship, learning, witness, service, support,* and *partnership* beyond the congregation. This exercise alone is often an "AHA!" experience for members. Then begin a process of developing objectives, goals, and strategies for each of the ministry areas for the coming year. Later, you can branch out to long-range planning.

3. Inspire confidence in the life of the congregation. Bishop Kenneth Sauer of the Evangelical Lutheran Church in America once said, "If you're not up on something, you're likely to be down on it." While going on to say that such a proverb cannot be taken to extremes, he noted that when people are aware of a ministry, they are more supportive. When they feel they are on the outside of the information isle, they begin to have reservations.

When people feel that they are part of something great, they want to give to it. An effective stewardship program can inspire a contagious enthusiasm—reminding people that the church is here for the right reasons. God is being served, and people are receiving the blessings of the Holy Spirit.

4. Encourage a concentrated look at personal giving. This "last but not least" ingredient in a successful stewardship campaign gives members the opportunity to reevaluate their personal financial commitment. The campaign itself may be the "dough," but asking people to consider the vital question is the "leaven" that turns a vision into the bread of ministry.

The vital question can be asked in many ways, but all members need to be given the opportunity to: (1) Reflect on the manner in which they have responded financially to God's saving grace during the past year. (2) Make an intentional decision about what their sacrificial involvement will be during the coming year. (3) Ask themselves, "How much will I grow in my giving during the coming twelve months?"

The Second Vital Element: Year-round Stewardship

If an effective stewardship campaign is the dough, then it is fair to say that a year-round approach to stewardship education is the butter and jam for the freshly baked bread. In a brief campaign, it is not possible to cover with integrity a subject as vast as stewardship. Talking about stewardship only once a year, at the time of the campaign, can also give the impression that it is not too important.

Year-round stewardship is rooted in the understanding that stewardship is a way of life—not just something that happens once a year in the annual campaign, but *every day*. A year-round approach is an effort to strengthen and support members of the congregation in their knowledge and understanding of their roles as God's stewards.

Benefits of Year-round Stewardship

Year-round stewardship brings at least three benefits to a congregation. First, it allows time to address the nonfinancial dimensions of stewardship more fully than during the congregational appeal. Many congregations, in addition to an "estimate of giving" card, receive a time-and-abilities survey, which serves as a nonfinancial commitment of willingness to be involved in specific ministries of the church. Such surveys inform members of the numerous ministries of the congregation and provide avenues for recruiting new blood for committees and other work groups. It is often preferable to receive these time-and-talent sheets two to three months after the financial estimates of giving are received.

This reminds people again that stewardship is more than money. It enables them to struggle again with their own sacrificial involvement in the congregation's ministry. And it prevents members from succumbing to the temptation to take an either/or approach—"I can't give much money, but I can give time." The gospel does not invite us to share *either* our time and abilities *or* our financial blessings. It calls us to share *both*.

One word of caution regarding time-and-abilities surveys: Make sure your congregation is as committed to *using* the time-and-abilities surveys as it is in asking people to fill them out. A pastor in Illinois, arriving in a new congregation, found that members resisted filling out the surveys. When he asked why, members told him, "We've done that for years, but no one ever takes action on the forms. They just lay in a drawer." The pastor promised that each person would be asked to do at least one thing they committed to do on the survey, at some time throughout the year. The church office then incorporated the sheets into a computerized data base and passed the information along to committee and governing board members.

Second verse, similar to the first: Year-round stewardship education enables members to connect the meaning of Christian stewardship to other ministries of the congregation. How is serving on a worship committee an act of stewardship? How is being involved in teaching Sunday school a part of my stewardship life? For many people, these may be givens. Others must be reminded that ministry, service, and stewardship have many parallels.

Action Possibility: After the stewardship committee develops its year-round calendar for stewardship, invite the members of all other committees to share in some way. One committee per month could demonstrate how its ministry reflects Christian stewardship. For example, during one month of the year, the evangelism committee could share the way stewardship and evangelism interface. A brief look at Ephesians 1:3-14 offers some valuable help here. Paul speaks of God's "plan" for the fullness of time (vs. 10). That plan is to gather up all things in Christ.

Later in the text, the apostle goes on to say that we too have an inheritance in that plan toward our redemption as God's own people. God's plan for the fullness of time is the redemption of the world. The word Paul uses for plan is a word that translates "stewardship." God's stewardship for the fullness of time is the redemption—the evangelization—of the world. If God's stewardship involves evangelism, then certainly our stewardship encompasses it as well. While the evangelistic efforts of a congregation need financial undergirding, the most important ingredient to an evangelizing church is the commitment of its members to tell the story of Christ's love. Evangelism involves the commitment of time and abilities as much as the commitment of money.

A third benefit of a year-round stewardship program is that it simplifies the follow-up to the annual appeal. A part of the stewardship committee's calendar for year-round stewardship education should include times to examine the congregation's income in relation to expectations, and to share that with the congregation. In spite of healthy campaigns, some congregations find that anticipated income may not be realized in full unless follow-up is done.

Action Possibility: Some follow-up tips might include: (1) Enclose a brief letter with the financial secretary's quarterly reports to families. (2) At certain times of the year, send a letter encouraging people to remember the church. One example would be a letter sent in anticipation of leaner summer months. (3) Include with the quarterly reports an occasional thank-you note from those who lead a specialized ministry, from a missionary, or from the pastor.

Components of Year-round Stewardship

Since year-round stewardship is a permanent part of the congregation's ministry, rather than a once-a-year effort, several components should be a regular part of the calendar.

Stewardship Education. This begins with the stewardship committee. Make Bible study a part of every meeting. Each month, ask one member to prepare a short presentation from a book or other study material.

Action Possibilities:
- Ask members of the stewardship committee to serve as teachers or speakers, to share children's sermons on stewardship. Scatter a half dozen of these sermons throughout a year. Stewardship stories for children will inspire adults as well.
- Invite other faithful members to offer stewardship stories periodically. Members often hear these as part of annual appeals, but why not hear such stories at other times of the year? They can be given as a stewardship talk or presented in written form in the newsletter, as the monthly stewardship article.
- A stewardship shelf in your church library can remind people of the spiritual and devotional role of stewardship.
- Clip quotes from good stewardship books and other sources for use in the church newsletter and worship bulletin.
- Use a bulletin board to communicate stewardship ideas.
- Develop a wish list of equipment or other items the church needs. After approval by the church governing

body, post the list in the narthex and print it in the newsletter.
• Skits and plays enable children to act out stories illustrated in stewardship tracts.

As part of the annual calendar for year-round stewardship, strive for one educational activity per month.

Ministry Interpretation. While education instructs and builds a foundation, interpretation provides the dazzle. Ministry interpretation clarifies how the exciting programs and activities of the church proclaim the gospel. Even the little things that members take for granted as regular features of church life demonstrate a faith active in love. But these "little things" cannot be noticed and appreciated unless they are shared in new and exhilarating ways.

Action Possibilities:
• Consider a "Because of Your Gifts" bulletin-insert series: "Because of Your Gifts" the hungry have food; "Because of Your Gifts" the gospel is proclaimed in Ethiopia; "Because of Your Gifts" oppressed and disadvantaged countries are hearing the gospel. Such inserts, if well done, can be exciting. The various units of denominations often prepare inserts that can enhance such a series.
• By organizing an annual "Mission Fair," representatives of various ministries can share what they are doing. These may include guest speakers, such as missionaries on leave or church officials.
• Prepare a "Program Budget" to provide a greater emphasis on ministry—rather than a budget that merely lists all the items on which the church spends money each year. Program budgets can be built around ministry areas, each of which points to one of the reasons for the congregation's existence.

Regular Reporting. Interpretation proclaims what is being done; reporting publishes what has been done. Regular reporting ensures that members of the congregation have the opportunity to learn about every activity and ministry. Rather than skipping the first six months, send quarterly reports to each family throughout the entire year.

Action Possibility: Computer-generated charts and graphs often help people get a better picture of the mission they accomplish. Congregations without a computer usually have members with access to one at their work or in their home. Decide what you want to say—then say it with pizzazz.

Regular Listening. Keeping the leadership informed is just as important as keeping the congregation informed. Leaders cannot communicate what they do not know. Staying in touch with member concerns douses fires while they are still but sparks. Members who feel that they really belong and are heard by the leadership have a higher morale.

Action Possibility: Consider conducting a nonfinancial "Every Member Visit" every few years. Use the visit to let the members know that the church cares about them. Build into the visit a time to share some of the congregation's mission story, and an opportunity for member families to share what is near and dear to them.

An Annual Vision for Ministry. One of the most useful tools for congregational communication, this annual vision can highlight the entire ministry of the congregation and excite members regarding service.

Action Possibility: See Appendix C for suggestions for a Congregational Vision for Ministry brochure.

Evaluation and Re-calendaring. No year is complete until it leads to a better next one. Evaluate the strengths and challenges of the year-round emphasis. Could some emphases be rearranged? Were they placed in the best month? How can changing the calendar next year enhance it? What did we do this year that we should leave out next year? What did we not do this year that we should add next year?

Pastor Robin sat at her desk. It was the "morning after," and she found that concentration eluded her. Every time she tried to concentrate on the calendar in front of her, she found her mind wandering back to yesterday. She was reeling with joy. She kept saying to herself over and over, "I still can't believe it. The third year was the best of all!"

At about 10:30, Helen, the financial secretary, stuck her head in Robin's office, smiling from ear to ear.

"Hi, Robin. Getting any work done?"

"No," Robin answered with a grin. "I still can't get over the response yesterday!"

"Yeah, I know," agreed Helen. "Me too! I keep thinking it's all a mistake. Who would have thought that our third year with the same program would net the best results of the three-year cycle. In fact, I went over the figures twice last night. The only error I found actually increased the results by a few cents!"

Pastor Robin shook her head. "It's amazing. Maybe my faith in people wasn't big enough. I've been doing some doodling here instead of filling out my daily priorities. The first year, we had a 25 percent increase over the previous year."

"I remember. That was your first year here too, Robin."

"The second year, we got 18 percent more. I'd have been delighted with 12 to 15 percent this year. Thirty percent blows my mind! The real kicker is that when you compound the actual increase from the first year, we've doubled our income in just three years!"

"That's right. Each year builds on the one before. What's your thinking about next year? When we started this campaign for the third year, you said it should be the last time we use it for at least a year or two. Do you still feel that way, or can we try it another year?"

"Most stewardship specialists will tell us that no congregation should risk a program more than two or three years at the most. After a time, even the best of programs grows old. Let's give it a rest next year and do something else. I've got a couple of thoughts jotted down in the stewardship file that we can talk about in our next meeting. I'd still prefer to rely on the experience of the experts."

"Well, I don't think anyone will argue with you, Robin. We've all enjoyed your leadership more than words could ever express. Besides, you've been the first pastor we've had in years who has been really comfortable with teaching stewardship. None of us would have thought to develop a year-round calendar. By the time you'd finished your second year here, stewardship was a household word. Best of all, it's now a beautiful word, signifying our response to God's love. I don't think we'll ever again hear anybody say, 'We don't talk about money in this church.'"

"Thanks be to God, and 'Amen' to that," replied Robin.

III

THE TOUR GUIDE'S ROLE

Dear Alan,

As you approach the conclusion of your seminary preparation, I am sure you are ready and eager to begin putting all you have learned to work. Let me assure you, my friend, that you are in my prayers, especially as you prepare for ordination and all that follows.

I was glad to receive your letter and especially glad that you asked for some "practical stewardship advice from a practicing pastor."

First, let me point out the practical background you already have. What you have learned in seminary has much to do with stewardship. So does what you have learned in church, in Sunday school, and at home. In one sense, stewardship is no different for pastors than for anyone else.

Stewardship is simply recognizing that all we are and all we have is a gift from God. We are entrusted with gifts—to care for those gifts, to manage them, and to employ them to serve God in the world.

You have no doubt heard that "stewardship is everything we do after we say, 'I believe.'" We live in a world that pays very much attention to "what you have." The more skill, the more wealth, the more influence you have, the greater your prestige and esteem in the eyes of many people. The Christian steward, on the other hand, is not so much concerned with "what you have" as with "what you do with it." As Jesus said, "Whoever would be greatest among you must be servant of all."

Before pastors address the question of stewardship professionally, they must come to terms with the matter personally. The most powerful stewardship resource we have as pastors is our own personal example. The most obvious place to begin our personal stewardship is tithing. We can count our money and figure 10 percent in our heads. In our home, we make it a little more challenging and give the first 12 percent of our income to the church. It is also a little more rewarding at the end of the year when we sit down and celebrate how abundantly God has blessed us and how the Holy Spirit has given us the faith to share our resources. Of course, the spirit of thanksgiving that results inspires us to recognize and manage all we have—as a gift.

When it comes to managing time and abilities as Christian stewards, the task is not quite so clear cut. The principles are the same. It's just that the results are not so readily measured.

Again, pastoral stewardship is first personal stewardship. For pastors, however, there are added considerations. The pastor is a steward and a leader of stewards. Example is the foremost tool in our "Leadership Kit." There are others.

Two assumptions play a very important part in my ministry as a leader of stewards. First, I assume that our members want to be good stewards. Some dismiss this as a statement of the obvious. But then we proceed to design stewardship ministries that are based on manipulation and guilt, or worse. Assuming that our members want to be good stewards means that everything about stewardship ministries will be respectful and honest. This has a most positive effect on building the partnership so essential to faithful stewardship for all members.

My second assumption is that those who want to be good stewards often do not know how. Do you see how that establishes the primary agenda for stewardship ministry? Education is what congregations need—not fund-raising gimmicks. Effective stewardship education always focuses on the need of the giver to give, not on the need of the church to receive. Stressing the basics of stewardship is a welcome refresher to mature stewards. It is also an opportunity for them to share their own example. For those still coming to terms with the basics—and there are such people in every congregation—the cornerstone must be in place before anything else can be built.

Alan, you are aware that there is much more to stewardship than I have been able to share in this brief space. There are some fine resources available. Our denominational stewardship packet, our stewardship staff people, continuing education opportunities, and much more waits for you. However, keep in mind that our personal example is the light that should not be kept under a basket. Our members genuinely want to be good stewards, even if some don't know how yet. These thoughts are the best "practical stewardship advice from a practicing pastor" I know.

Thank you again, Alan, for asking about stewardship. Your concern to learn is the first step in effective stewardship ministry. God bless you and keep you, dear friend, as you answer the Holy Spirit's call to serve the gospel.

Sincerely in Christ,
Steve[3]

The Pastor's Leadership

Alan's desire for some "practical stewardship advice from a practicing pastor" is very common. When pastors leave those hallowed halls of seminary learning for the world of ministry, stewardship is one aspect of ministry that often evokes quivers and quakes. The vast majority of pastors in America today look back and shudder at how naive they were about stewardship when they entered the ministry. Many thought that if they faithfully preached the gospel, the money would come pouring in. Not So! Stewardship does not happen automatically. Christian stewardship, as with the mission and ministry it empowers, happens by design. Intentional groundwork, education, grooming, and leadership are the keys that unlock the door.

The pastor is the chief steward of the congregation. Congregations that are above the national average in their giving have one of several things in common. One of the most important of these is *strong pastoral leadership*.[4] In congregations with effective stewardship, the pastors give leadership to the stewardship ministry in at least four ways.

1. The pastor's life sets an example. Denominational leaders point out that they can track pastors by the footprints they leave behind in the congregations they serve. Most pastors leave congregations much the way they found them, with some changes and improvements. Some leave congregations in much better health than they found them: more members, better attendance, higher levels of commitment, better giving, and more community service. This continues to happen in one congregation after another. But some pastors seem to have the opposite kind of gifts. No matter what the congregations are like when they arrive, things go downhill and the churches are better off when they leave. Their primary contribution is their absence.

The pastor is the key to effective stewardship and ministry. If stewardship becomes a way of life in the congregation, the pastor will lead the way.

2. The pastor's words set an example. An Ohio pastor first witnessed to his giving by accident. Not a planned part of his sermon, he mentioned his giving in an impromptu remark. He later discovered that five of the most generous

40

families in the congregation increased their giving the very next week. While a pastor's influence is seldom that dramatic or instantaneous, this incident illustrates the power of a pastor's personal example.

Rather than merely informing the congregation of the amount of money given through the church, however, most pastors find it more effective to share their "stewardship story." Pastors usually have had to struggle with their budgets and incomes as much or more than the members. Nor are pastors any more immune than lay people to struggles in their faith commitment. Honesty and transparency at these points help people realize that pastors too are human beings who struggle with life and all its challenges.

Some pastors and lay professionals are hesitant at this point. These "reluctant witnesses" fall into four groups: (1) Some take the attitude that this type of witnessing would seem like bragging. Realizing that pastors are often among the top 10 percent of the givers in their congregations, they hesitate to identify themselves in this way. (2) Others feel that since giving is a very personal thing, it should not be discussed publicly. (3) A smaller percentage of pastors do not share their giving because they are personally embarrassed to do so. Some have just finished four years of college and four more years of seminary, face a debt of $50,000, and are beginning a job that often pays less than they would be earning if they had begun working right after high school. They may even be striving to grow toward a tithe, but feel that this is "impossible" just now. (4) Sadly, some pastors and church professionals—like some laypeople—have not grown to realize the importance of financial giving in their own Christian lives. They may rationalize this behavior by suggesting that their whole lives are sacrificially given to the Lord. Therefore they ask themselves, "Why should I also be expected to give sacrificially of my financial resources?"

How, then, do people in these four groups answer the big question: *Should we tell, or should we not tell?* All things considered, the answer must be a resounding **"Yes!"**

The objections of these hesitant witnesses have little merit. First, consider the difference between boasting and giving witness. God calls all Christians to give witness to their faith and their commitment. Financial stewardship is one of our primary opportunities to make a difference by sharing our witness.

Second, while Christian stewardship is a very personal matter, it is not a private affair. As in so many other aspects of our faith, keeping our stewardship private means that we are removing part of its influential effectiveness.

Third, cannot those who are not yet tithers merely give witness to their commitment to grow toward a tithe?

Finally, we can see the flaw in logic of the person who says, "I can give time but not money." Scripture does not give us a choice among time, talents, and treasure. How can a pastor credibly say that God calls him or her to exclude one of these from personal stewardship commitment?

Action Possibility: Undertake a study of Christian stewardship within your local ministerial group. Discuss the pros and cons of sharing your stewardship story with the congregation. Find out how many clergy colleagues already speak directly with their congregations about their giving. Ask what benefits they feel both they and their congregations receive by such openness.

3. The pastor's stewardship education sets an example. The pastor's role as stewardship leader includes the vocation of teacher, and a teacher's first duty is not to inform, but to inspire. A pastor is not merely a walking textbook filled with facts neatly arranged for dictation, but a dynamo charged with a contagious enthusiasm for our stewardship mandate. Information tells people what to do. Inspiration helps them want to do it. Strong stewardship education does both. The pastor delivers this package in several ways.

First, the pastor is the chief Bible teacher and theologian of the church. Communicating a biblical understanding of stewardship is far stronger than merely saying, "This is what

I think about money." Failing to include this element of stewardship education usually means failing entirely.

If an interviewer from National Public Radio could talk to Joseph, the reporter might ask, "Joseph, what does it mean to you to be a steward? You've been through some pretty rough times. You were kidnapped by your brothers and sold as a slave. You wound up in Egypt and eventually became a steward in the home of Potipher. Tell us, Joseph, what does it mean to be a steward?"

The great Hebrew with the coat of many colors might have responded, "It means to be trusted. My boss trusted me with everything he had. He told me that I had the run of the house, and he gave me the authority to do business in his name. For me, it meant to live up to that trust, even when he didn't think that I was. I was an honest steward. I handled his money faithfully and made him even richer. My stewardship charge was really from God. Living up to that stewardship is what my whole life was all about."

Action Possibility: Both Old and New Testaments teem with rich examples of stewardship. If Christians could read their Bibles with stewardship-tinted glasses, they would discover hundreds of models. In a pastor's Sunday school class, provide a series of lessons called "The Stewardship Connection." Invite members to find the unexpected stewardship connections in numerous Bible stories. Many passages not normally associated with stewardship reveal surprising stewardship lessons.

Second, the pastor is the church's chief planning facilitator. Pastors in most denominations receive a small tree's worth of paper every year. Many church bodies, for example, provide an annual resource packet of stewardship materials. Included are numerous resources that may be shared with committees. Helping a committee to find its way through the crevices and gorges of these mountains of available stewardship materials and ideas is an essential element of the pastor's leadership role.

The most powerful aspect of this guidance will come from asking the right questions. What type of path is best this year? What are we trying to accomplish with our entire stewardship ministry and appeal? The logical answer is more money for mission, but the pastor can keep the issue from being dropped there. While growth in giving is important to maintaining growth in mission, it is only one reason a congregation needs an annual stewardship appeal. Of equal importance is the spiritual growth of each member which comes from growth in stewardship. The pastor's leadership can help people catch the vision of going to new regions where they "have never gone before" and look forward to the trip. Stewardship apart from mission is as uninviting as stagnant water. When mission and spiritual growth is the focus, stewardship becomes a stream flowing in the desert. The pastor, as planning facilitator, adds the pragmatic wheels to the biblical engine.

4. *The pastor's biblical teachings of percentage giving and tithing set an example.* Paul charged Christians to give an amount in proportion to their income. Tithing, giving 10 percent of one's income, is a guide for giving accepted by millions of Christians. It has historic roots in Holy Scripture, with frequent references in the Old Testament. Yet, only about 22 percent of the members of churches in the U.S.A. are tithers.[5] And only a slightly larger percentage of members seem to practice percentage giving of any kind; figures range from 30 to 40 percent. Even more alarming, only about 50 percent even knew what percentage of their income they give.[6] In view of these statistics, pastors seem in little danger of overstressing biblical teaching regarding the tithe and percentage of giving.

Some point out that the New Testament record contains few tithing verses and that Jesus did not make this a major focus. While that is true, there is no reference to Christ ever suggesting any standard *less* than a tithe. Jesus probably seldom referred to tithing because such teachings were unnecessary. Jesus and his followers were raised in the Jewish tradition. They simply accepted tithing as a basic standard of religious behavior and went on from there. While Jesus' only specific recorded comment regarding the tithe (Matt. 23:23) is more of a back-door affirmation than a direct commendation, it illustrates his assumptions about giving: "Woe to you, scribes and Pharisees, hypocrites! For you tithe mint, dill, and cummin, and have neglected the weightier matters of the law: justice and mercy and faith. It is these you ought to have practiced *without neglecting the others* [the tithes]" (emphasis added).

Sunday lunch had hardly begun when Karl said to his wife, "Tess, Pastor Glen's sermon kind of hit me between the eyes today."

"Oh? How do you mean, Karl?"

"Well, I've always thought we were pretty good givers to our church. When I was financial secretary several years ago, I discovered that we were among the top three givers in the congregation. I think I used that knowledge to pat myself on the back for a job well done."

"And after today, you think you're not such a good steward after all?" Tess wondered.

"Well, I don't think I'd go that far," Karl answered, "but I feel as if I've forgotten that it's part of the Christian life to grow in all parts of Christian living. We've been involved in Bible studies to grow in our commitment to Christ. We've served on several committees of the church. But I've never once asked if I should give more this year than I did last year. I was waiting for some of the other members to catch up."

"You know, honey, our combined income is considerably more than that of some of our other members!"

"Right, but what really got me was when Pastor Glen, without seeming to brag at all, mentioned the amount he and Margaret give."

"I thought the same. And she's not even working full-time."

45

"It was obvious that they give more than a tithe of their income. And to top that off, he commented that they were still trying to grow by one percent of their income per year. That really hit home. I did some mental calculations, and I'm ashamed to admit that we're only giving about four percent to the Lord's work."

"Darling, maybe it's time we took the risk and started tithing. After all, we can afford it. There are many who have not had the blessings God has given us. I think we need to say a stronger thank you to God for what we have received, don't you?"

"I do," responded Karl. "In fact, I think we should start next Sunday. It may be a little tight until we adjust some things, but we can do it. Is that okay with you?"

"I think that's just fine. Are you going to tell Pastor Glen about our decision?"

"You bet. I think maybe it's good for the pastor to know that I listen to his sermons, at least once in a while. Besides, this feels so good, I've just got to share it. Maybe we should even let him tell others that at least one family has decided to grow."

"Why don't you give him a call right after lunch, honey?"

"I've got a better idea. Let's jump in the car and drive over to the parsonage and tell him in person."

No, the stewardship leadership of pastors does not exert this kind of influence *every* time he or she speaks. But no other person in the church has this type of influential opportunity. At the bottom line we see a clear fact: Members of a tour group seldom go where their tour guide has not already been.

IV

TO PLEDGE OR NOT TO PLEDGE: THAT IS THE QUESTION

"Hi, George," said Nancy as she sat down across from him in the fellowship hall. "Interesting sermon today, wasn't it?"

"Yeah, it was pretty good . . . for a stewardship sermon," George replied with a sheepish smile. "Just kidding. It was good, but there was one part I've always had difficulty with."

"Oh, what was that?"

"When the pastor talked about pledging. I won't disagree that pledging may help the congregation do a better job of planning the budget for next year. But I guess I'm just not convinced that pledging is a good thing."

"Inquiring minds want to know! Why's that, George?"

"I've always figured that what I give is between God and me. Giving is a very personal thing for me. Now, it's no secret that I'm a tither. I've long advocated tithing as a reasonable response to God's love. But if I put that amount on a piece of paper, someone is going to be able to figure out my income."

"George, tell me. If the shoe was on the other foot—if you were the one who was tabulating the pledges, would you calculate someone's income?"

"Heavens no!" he exclaimed. "I wouldn't think of it."

"Then what makes you think someone else would? But that's not the only reason you don't want to pledge, is it?"

"No, I guess another reason is that my income isn't always terribly secure. I keep thinking that if it changes, I may not be able to keep up my pledge."

"Did you get a chance to read the newsletter that came out last week?" asked Nancy.

"No, mine didn't arrive until the end of the week, and I just didn't have time to look through it. Why?"

"There's an excellent article from Pastor Julie in it about that very concern. She's aware that people often feel that way. In the congregation where she did her internship, they had even quit referring to them as pledges. Instead, they used the term *estimate of giving*. That helped people realize they were not signing a contract with the church and that if something happened, it was okay. Christian people love to give, and they will usually give what they estimate, unless something really bad happens. She suggested that we should erase the word *pledge* from our vocabulary and insert *estimate of giving*. I think she was right. After all, we don't send out bills to anyone who gets behind.

"She also pointed out something else important. People who estimate their giving usually give more than those who don't. Now, I know that since you're a tither, and your pledge—sorry, estimate—would be what you're giving now, that's not true for you. But remember, only about 20 percent of our congregation tithes. Besides, who said we have to stop growing when we reach a tithe?"

"Well, you really know how to hit the nail on the head, Nancy. But you're right. I have thought of a tithe as fulfilling my commitment. Maybe it's time I thought about growing. After all, we don't want to stop reading God's Word when we've read 10 percent of the Bible, do we?"

"Then you'll try pledging—oops—estimating?"
"Yes, Nancy, you've been a good teacher. Thank you."

Nearly everyone makes a pledge or estimate of their giving. Many just do not put it on paper. But if they do not write it in black and white, their pledge is usually much smaller. If they will not make a written commitment, odds are that they have not given it serious, prayerful consideration. "I'll give but I won't pledge," often means:
- "I'll give, but you won't need to make any special trips to the bank for same-day deposits."
- "I have no plan for giving that I am willing to put on paper." (This also means, "Giving isn't that important in my life.")
- "I don't really believe in the mission and ministry of my church."
- "I'll give something, but I won't grow in my giving."

Exceptions do exist, of course. There are mature Christians and mature stewards in every congregation who give stewardship the priority it deserves. And there are a few members who are unwilling to estimate their giving, but who are among the top givers in the congregation. But such exceptions are rare and usually number only one or two families in the congregation.

Congregations with high levels of giving realize that people who estimate their giving (pledge) do give more. Studies indicate that members who make estimates of their giving usually give at least 30 percent more than those who do not estimate. In one study, the numerous factors that interconnect in determining members' giving levels resulted in the following percentages:
- Congregations that asked members to estimate their giving had 30.2 percent higher average giving levels than those not using written commitments.
- Congregations that had an annual stewardship emphasis had 23.3 percent higher giving levels than those with no annual appeal.

- Congregations that asked members to consider tithing reported 19.6 percent higher giving levels than those that did not mention tithing.
- Congregations that used all three of these activities had 38.5 percent higher giving levels than those that used none of them.[7]

Why Estimate Giving?

If a seminary debate team were to argue the pros and cons of estimating giving, the hands-down winner would have to be the pros. For every reason that a person can invent for not estimating giving, there are several better reasons for doing so. Congregations that experience growing incomes and do effective outreach know that estimates of giving are an important factor. Christians who estimate their giving know the need of the giver to grow. Every congregation recognizes its responsibility to help people grow in faith and disciple-ship. Growth in giving often enables and augments growth in other areas of the Christian life.

Maebelle approached her pastor after their congregation's first-ever stewardship appeal. She reached out and clasped his hands in hers.

"Pastor, I want to tell you something," she beamed. "When you first started this stewardship stuff, I had some reservations."

"I take it from the look on your face that perhaps they've been dispelled by now, Maebelle," he replied.

"Indeed they have," she chuckled. "Not only have I been set free to be a better steward, I feel that I'm growing in the rest of my Christian life too. Even our weekly Bible studies seem to mean more. I can't thank you enough for helping this old bird find a few new seeds."

Such stories are common when people catch the vision to grow in their giving. Paul writes, in Ephesians 2:8-9, "For by grace you have been saved through faith, and this is not your own doing; it is the gift of God—not the result of works, so that no one may boast." Grace is the God-given, undeserved love that enriches our earthly lives and brings wholeness. God's grace reaches out to us, even when we feel unreachable, and moves us to a firm commitment to Jesus Christ. God's grace virtually compels a response; for how can even the most callous heart not respond to love such as this? Grace draws from us a firm commitment to contribute a portion of our time, our abilities, and the dollar resources God has showered upon us.

Making a written estimate of giving can be important to Christians for at least ten reasons.

1. Estimating risks in faith; it reflects the need to put God first. Martin Luther once said that every Christian goes through three conversions in life—first, the heart, then the head, and finally the purse. For God to be really first in the lives of Christians, all three are necessary. Many Christians find that the last to be converted, the last to be committed to the Lord, is our wealth.

One of the most insidious addictions in our society often traps even the most dedicated Christian people. Wealth addiction does not convince us that wealth is the most important priority in life. It merely suggests that it is one of the most important. This addiction does not suggest to us that God should be in second place. It does not even place wealth above God. What it does is subtly place wealth equal with God. It creates a pantheon with two gods at the top— God and money. But we cannot serve God and money.

Estimating our giving makes God the God of our lives, not just the God of our church. Growing in our commitment each year gives external evidence of our internal priorities. We put God first. We risk in faith. We trust in God to provide. And we are thereby healed from addiction to wealth.

2. Estimating acknowledges that God asks for our commitment. Jesus emphasized the need for commitment to

Godly priorities: "But strive first for the kingdom of God and his righteousness, and all these things will be given to you as well" (Matt. 6:33). When Peter piously pointed out that the disciples had left everything to follow Jesus, the Lord replied, "Truly I tell you, there is no one who has left house or brothers or sisters or mother or father or children or fields, for my sake and for the sake of the good news, who will not receive a hundredfold now in this age . . . and in the age to come eternal life" (Mark 10:29-30).

God asks not just that we give—but that we be committed to justice and mercy and faith in all the world. As Christians, our estimate of giving is foundational to all ministry. An estimate helps our church plan for and provide ministry.

3. Estimating emphasizes that God is vital to our lives. Our personal support of the Lord's ministry is a way to make a difference in the world. Our estimates of giving provide a public witness to the role God plays in our lives.

Dr. Paul Wee, a staff member of the Lutheran World Federation, told about standing at the bedside of dying Archbishop Janis Matulis of Latvia. A visitor had just sung, at Matulis' request, an old spiritual with the words, "Oh, when I am alone, when I am alone, give me Jesus." Matulis then asked:

> Do you know why this song means so much to me? Three times war passed over Latvia, killing two-fifths of our people. They burned down my church and destroyed the Bibles and hymnals. They took away my wife, and I never saw her again. When it was all gone, I realized that I had nothing else in this world but Jesus Christ. It was like a breath of freedom. From that moment on, I learned how to use whatever came my way—little bits of medicine left over, a piece of coal, apples, spices—so that somehow the sacrament of God's love would be shared with the larger community because of Jesus Christ.[8]

4. Making an estimate frees. Diana met her husband while they were attending the same seminary. He was from a different denomination and was taking some additional courses while serving a nearby country church. After a time they married, serving a few miles from each other in congregations of their respective denominations. When a discussion of giving came up, the couple realized that their varied traditions brought different assumptions. His had been a tithing tradition, so for him, the decision of what to give was very simple. The congregation in which Diana grew up, however, had never emphasized the tithe, and the idea was somewhat new to her. So strong was his commitment to tithe that she simply agreed to do so.

She said later, "For the first time in my life, I found that I was free in my giving. There was no longer the struggle about what to give. God would receive the first 10 percent automatically. Anything we could give beyond that would be icing on the cake."

Many Christians affirm that one of the best things about both tithing and estimating their giving is that they win a sense of freedom. They are free because they are giving as God has blessed them. They are free because they know God receives the percentage or tithe they have committed as a reflection of their spiritual commitment. They are freed to concentrate on other service to God, knowing that their financial commitment for the coming year clears other competing priorities out of the way.

5. Christians lead by example. A young man from South Africa approached a minister who had been a guest speaker at a university seminar. The young man introduced himself by saying, "I am from South Africa, and I would like to ask you what for me is a very important question.

"I have lived in a land where my family and I have been persecuted, starved, and tortured. My people have been oppressed for many years. We have seen times when we didn't know if other family members were alive or dead. Poverty was for us a way of life. Children died for lack of food. I was imprisoned for no apparent reason and tortured. Later I escaped, and with the help of several courageous people, I came here to America. My question is this. Please understand that I am not asking it to put you down, but to discover the answer. How can you, a rich Christian from America who has never experienced any of these things, say to me, a man from South Africa, 'Jesus loves you'?"

The speaker was grateful that the question had taken so long to ask.

He responded, "You are, of course, right. I have never lived in any land where I have been persecuted. I have always had food to eat. I don't honestly know by experience the meaning of hunger. My family has never been tortured or murdered. I honestly don't know how I would respond if they were. This is all I can say. I have experienced the love and intervention of Jesus Christ in my life. I share with you what God has done for me. And I hope, I pray, that even though the words may sound hollow, that when you hear me say, 'Jesus loves you' that you also see that Jesus loves you through my actions and my faith."

Our lives are a magnifying glass through which people see either Christ or something else. The only way many people will ever experience the gospel is through Christians. If our words proclaim our faith and our whole life is exemplary, but we fail to illustrate an effective stewardship of the gifts God has entrusted to us, will that witness stand up under scrutiny?

Jesus set the example in stewardship. Christ was not afraid to be nailed to the cross. Christians, therefore, should not be afraid to affix their names to estimates of giving for God's work. An estimate is an outward expression of our love for God.

6. Estimating reflects our disciplined response to Christ's love. Dietrich Bonhoeffer, a prisoner of the Third Reich who spoke out against Nazism, discussed the meaning of a disciplined Christian life. He wrote about the difference between "cheap grace" and "costly grace." Cheap grace merely accepts the gifts of God without any real depth of commitment.

Cheap grace is the deadly enemy of our Church. Cheap grace means grace sold at the market. Cheap grace means grace as a doctrine, a principle, a system. Cheap grace is the preaching of forgiveness without requiring repentance, baptism without church discipline, communion without confession, absolution without personal confession. Cheap grace is grace without discipline, grace without the cross, grace without Jesus Christ, living and incarnate.

Contrasted with this cheap grace is what Bonhoeffer called costly grace:

Such grace is costly because it calls us to follow, and it is grace because it calls us to follow Jesus Christ. It is costly because it costs us our life, and it is grace because it gives the only true life. It is costly because it condemns sin, and grace because it justifies the sinner. Above all, it is costly because it cost God the life of his Son, and what has cost God so much cannot be cheap for us.[9]

The discipline of making an estimate and sticking to it is a direct response to a loving God who paid for our life in full, on Calvary. The sharing of our estimate of giving is one way to respond to the gift of life. It does not take for granted the grace of God.

7. Estimating begets ministry. Jesus' feeding of the five thousand (John 6:1-15) started with an offering. Ministry to the crowd began when the disciples brought five loaves and two fish. In the same way, the offering of Jesus' life on the cross began the ministry of redemption. Consistent with this pattern, Paul called on the people of the ancient world to make an offering to minister to the starving, persecuted people of Judea. Countless other biblical examples demonstrate that giving is not just for the spiritual growth of the giver; it results in ministry.

8. Estimating enables the church to plan. Picture yourself about to embark on a cross-country trip. Before leaving, you probably will make some plans. You will check a road atlas or map to determine the major highways you want to travel. You may even obtain a "trip-tick." You will probably have your car checked over, the oil changed, and determine whether the hoses are in good condition. You are also likely to check to see if you have enough money to pay for gas, food, and lodging.

Every congregation embarks on a journey each year. That journey involves some planning for ministry, and, we hope, undertaking some new challenges. A vision for ministry with no challenges is nearsighted vision. Estimating our giving enables the church to get an accurate picture of income for the coming year, so that leaders can plan their ministries by using a rational roadmap.

9. An estimate is not a contract. Horror stories abound about congregations that have misused and abused "pledges." During the Great Depression of the 1930s, one congregation sold its pledges to a local bank at 90 percent of face value. A few congregations have sent out bills and over-due notices to members who were behind on their commitments. Some have even tried to "assess" their members for specific projects. It is no small wonder that in some congregations, the word pledge holds bitter memories.

We should view our estimate of giving as a personal commitment that flows from our love for Christ. Most Christians want to give. Thus, this estimate is a voluntary commitment given freely and openly. Churches should therefore avoid regarding estimates as legally binding promissory notes. Rather, they express a Christian's hopes and cares for the programs of ministry that proclaim Christ's love in the world. They are more like birthday gifts than bank-loan notes.

10. An estimate enables intentional decisions. Christians who fail to make an intentional decision about their giving often find that careful examination of their stewardship reveals that they are "bucking" the Lord. Lack of an intentional decision usually begets lower giving. People who toss a "buck" or even a "few bucks" into the offering plate are hardly conscientious stewards. Such people are usually giving God a token of their leftovers—what is left after the bills are paid. Biblical stewardship involves first-fruits giving— giving off the top. Estimates enable members to be truly intentional about their personal stewardship.

Tips for (Re)Introducing Estimates

Even as a new pastor right out of seminary, Beverly knew better, but knowing sometimes takes a back seat to *urgency*. Bev's new congregation had not experienced any form of estimates of giving for the previous seven years. Her predecessor had been a bit uncomfortable with "pledging," by any name.

Beverly, on the other hand, was very comfortable with the idea, though she sensed a bit of difficulty with those who failed to see the connection between commitment and giving. At her first governing board meeting, she suggested that "things would be a lot better" if both tithing and pledging were reintroduced as household words.

A few of the "more experienced" members of the board listened with considered courtesy. They then moved to table the idea until Beverly could bring a plan for making the introduction. After the meeting, Dorothy, who was afraid that the new pastor was feeling "stepped on" took her aside.

"Pastor," she began, "I hope you didn't feel too disappointed that we didn't jump right into your plan to reintroduce pledging. Perhaps we handled the motion to table a little too abruptly."

"I won't deny that I was a bit hurt at first," replied Beverly. "I thought perhaps I had said something to offend someone."

"Not at all. But you see, many members find change difficult. You're a new pastor, and you're also the first woman to serve as our pastor. That's a big change in itself. Many of us on the board are aware that change is difficult for some of our members and that we have to make changes in small steps, rather than in giant leaps."

Beverly smiled. "I should have known better."

Dorothy went on, "You're excited about getting things rolling, and that's great. Perhaps we can get together and come up with a plan to reintroduce pledging to present to our next board meeting. I'll be glad to help."

Introducing or reintroducing estimates of giving in congregations can often be a challenge equivalent to climbing the north face of the Matterhorn. Congregations and pastors who would climb that mountain need to consider the terrain. Unlike climbing the Matterhorn, introducing or reintroducing pledging need not be insurmountable if three steps are kept in mind.

Check the equipment. What do we have on hand that will help us in our journey? When the trip involves introducing a stewardship concept, one might call these pieces of equipment the givens. Several stewardship facts can be classified as givens. First, people like to give. Second, Christians are willing to grow in their giving if asked. Third, members like to know and need to know where their money is going. Fourth, people are more willing to estimate their giving if we keep it nonthreatening and voluntary.

Identify potential hazards. Where on our climb are we most likely to encounter hazards? Are they easily overcome, or will it take additional time and effort? The introduction of estimates of giving encounters similar questions. The first might be, "Is there genuine resistance to pledging?" A second might be, "What are the reasons for, and the scope of, the resistance?" Sometimes getting to the bottom of an issue involves asking questions in order to answer questions.

- Has there been a bad experience with estimates of giving, or knowledge of someone who has had a bad experience? War stories about pledging are often as embellished as the proverbial fish stories. The more they are told, the bigger they get. Stories that depict the real joy of giving tend to get less press.

- Is resistance related to fear? What is the basis for such fear? Some people are afraid to make an estimate of their giving because they are afraid they may not be able to live up to it. Counter such fears by allowing people to express them. There may be another member who has overcome the same fear. If so, that person may be able to help others over the crags.
- Is resistance related to the word *pledge?* If so, consider explaining what is meant by a pledge to the church. Consider changing the term to avoid the stereotype.
- Is resistance a spiritual problem? A spiritual problem might include the inability to connect giving with Christian commitment. For Christians who have not yet grown to active discipleship, the church must seek ways to help them grow.
- What is the scope of the resistance? Not everyone resists. And not everyone makes an estimate. Even in congregations where pledging is practiced, only about 50 percent of the members make an estimate. This does not mean that the other 50 percent is totally resistant. Frequently, the only real resistance is found in two or three loud voices that prevail because no one is willing to stand up to them.

Begin the ascent. The Matterhorn is beautiful, but admiring its beauty will not get a person one foot higher than the lodge. After all the preliminary preparations are made, the climb must begin. Pastor Beverly would be wise to plan a step-by-step approach to introducing the concept of pledging to her members. Considering the discoveries from the above questions, she will present her governing board with an approach to helping people take that first step of faith toward responsible, joy-filled pledging.

As a pastor greeted his members at the door following a

stewardship sermon in which he had discussed pledging, a rather disgruntled member asked accusingly, "Where in the Bible do you find anything about pledging?"

Not too surprised at the man's question, the pastor replied, "That's a good question, John. Let's get together over lunch and talk about it this week."

Disarmed by the pastor's cordiality, the man's tone changed. "Well, I guess that'd be all right," he responded.

"Fine, how about Tuesday, around noon? I'll pick you up, and we can go from your place."

After they had ordered, the pastor brought up the subject. "You know, your question was a good one. It forced me to do some heavy thinking on my day off yesterday. At first, I racked my brain, trying to find a prooftext. Then it occurred to me that I was working too hard. The Bible is full of references to pledging."

"Come on now, Pastor. I'm not surprised that you can find a reference to pledging that I don't know about. But to say that the Bible is full of talk about pledging goes a little far, don't you think?"

"No, and I think you'll agree," replied the pastor.

"Now you've got my curiosity up," said John. "Okay, give it your best shot."

"The first thing I did was sit down and boot up my word processor. I typed in the word *pledge* and called up the thesaurus. All kinds of biblical terms appeared before my eyes. Here's just part of the list." The pastor showed John a page with several words written on it: *Commit, Promise, Dedicate, Devote, Covenant, Vow.*

"You see, John, when we *commit* our lives to Jesus Christ, we *promise* that we will *dedicate* our entire lives to serve God. We *devote* the rest of our lives to the *covenant* God made with us in Jesus Christ. When we were brought into the family of God, we *vowed* that we would serve our Lord for the rest of our lives."

"I think I'm beginning to understand what you're getting at, Pastor," said John. "But I'm not real sure that I see how this fits in with my pledge to give a dollar amount to the church each year. I understand the commitment I made when I was confirmed, but how does that relate to my giving?"

The pastor took a sip of coffee and continued, "I think you'll agree that all the words on this sheet of paper have to do with our spiritual commitment to Christ, right?"

"Right."

"Christian stewardship, and specifically the focused part of stewardship which relates to the giving of our tithes and offerings, is merely a reflection of our spiritual commitment to Christ. Stewardship is first of all our response to God. It is God's gift of Jesus Christ as our Savior that triggers our commitment. Christians are called to grow in grace and knowledge of the truth. We expect that we will grow spiritually every year. We want to have a better understanding of Scripture next year than we do this year. That's the reason you asked the question you did on Sunday. You wanted to know how the two connected."

"You're being a bit too generous with your interpretation of my question. I think I was feeling a bit defensive and therefore took the *offensive*. But thank you, and I have grown as a result of your kind response to a rather caustic question. I think I owe you an apology."

"None necessary," responded the pastor. "When a Christian raises a concern about the Scriptures, it's always an opportunity to grow. As we make our estimate of giving (what you called a *pledge*), we are renewing our covenant with God. We are committing ourselves to being intentional about our stewardship of the financial blessings God has given us. The side benefit is that we expect to grow spiritually in the coming year, even as we grow in our giving."

"Pastor, I have a request."

"Sure, what is it?"

"May I have the privilege of joining in a stewardship talk this Sunday? I'd like to share with the whole congregation what I've discovered here. And I'd like to openly acknowledge that I've changed my mind. Next Sunday, I will make my first financial pledge ever. We're never too old to grow."

V

BUILD FROM BLUEPRINTS

The Reverend Mark Tweedle, D.D., sat in the office of Fading Glory Church with the members of the stewrdship committee. Everyone was there except Bill, the chair of the committee.

Leonard Sharp, the congregation's treasurer, asked, "Have you talked with Bill this week, Reverend?"

"Well no, Leonard, but on his way out of church on Sunday he said he'd see me tonight. I don't know if—" The phone interrupted him in mid-sentence.

"Hello, Fading Glory Church. How may I be of service?" the pastor answered pleasantly.

"Reverend, this is Carla, Bill's wife. Bill just phoned me from Phoenix to say that when he was called out of town on Monday, he forgot to let you know he couldn't make the stewardship committee meeting. Could you cover for him?"

"That's got to be Bill's wife, saying he's going to miss another meeting," groused Leonard to Lizzy Faire.

Lizzy, an older woman who practically idolized Reverend Tweedle and every other pastor, wrinkled her nose at him, telegraphing her disapproval of his cynical attitude.

"Leonard," she commented in a motherly tone, "you should learn to be a little more tolerant with people."

The pastor hung up the phone and looked sheepishly at Willis Nerdlinger. "Bill's in Phoenix, Willis. As vice-chair, I guess it falls to you to start our meeting."

Glowing at this grand opportunity to serve, Willis drew himself to his full stature and called the meeting to order. But almost immediately, a blank expression appeared on his face and he turned to the pastor.

"What do I do now?"

"Let's open with prayer," responded the pastor. "If you like, I'll be glad to lead us."

Within a millisecond of the "Amen," Leonard began: "It seems to me that we've got a big evening cut out for us. It's already September, and we haven't even decided what appeal to use this fall. Since we usually do our budget in October and our stewardship campaign in November, we'd better get crackin'. I think it was a big mistake to cancel our summer meetings."

"Maybe it would have been best to meet, Len," gushed Lizzy, "but I feel certain that our beloved pastor has some great ideas. What do you suggest, Reverend Tweedle?"

"I do have one suggestion we might try," the pastor responded thoughtfully. "At a workshop I attended recently, the leader mentioned that many churches that have their appeal *after* they plan the budget would do better to reverse the order. I thought perhaps this year we should consider that."

"Little late for that, isn't it?" asked Len. "After all, that would mean we'd have to get something ready in the next two weeks."

"I guess you're right," agreed the pastor, blanching a bit at having his only suggestion shot down in one sentence.

"I know! I know!" blurted Lizzy. "I think we need the pastor to preach one of those inspirational sermons on stewardship."

"Better be careful, though, pastor," cautioned Chairman (pro tem) Nerdlinger. "We don't want to offend anybody just before we ask them to grow in their giving."

"Whaddaya mean, *grow?*" asked Lizzy in astonishment. "I think everyone in our church is doing their very best."

"Humph! I doubt that," Leonard objected. "You should see some of the pitiful checks that come in. Pastor, wouldn't it be a good idea if we shopped around and bought one of those printed campaigns this year? At least that would give us some idea of where to start."

"Oh, I don't know, Len," responded the pastor. "Some people don't like those canned programs. Maybe we should just send out a couple of letters, announce a pledge Sunday, and hope for the best."

"I think that sounds great," Lizzy agreed enthusiastically. "After all, I think it's important that we not interrupt people's life-styles any more than necessary."

Congregations with high levels of giving are aware that effective stewardship needs careful planning and careful execution of that plan. Skimping on the stewardship appeal usually means skimping on ministry. With countless excellent programs available, congregations are well advised to use one of them. Professionally prepared stewardship appeals have two advantages over campaigns planned and executed by a stewardship committee.

First, they have been written by stewardship specialists and have been tried and tested. If instructions are carefully followed, most will work in nearly every congregation.

Second, following a prepared program helps avoid having committee members perform surgery on the campaign—and accidentally cut out its heart while attempting an appendectomy.

Stewardship is one of those disciplines in which people, left to their own devices, almost always choose the easiest way (and therefore the least effective way). What happened at Fading Glory Church, unfortunately, is not far from reality in many congregations. Time slips away. The month for the annual stewardship emphasis creeps up, with no plans underway.

"But we did that last year!" or "We already know that!" are just two of the excuses for taking shortcuts. Often, when the stewardship committee says it used a campaign that didn't work, a little "fishing" will reveal that the members performed major surgery on the program. When a well-structured program fails, it usually is because a vital organ has been removed.

Step One: The Appeal

Leaders who are determining the type of appeal to use should consider several questions: (1) What has the congregation done in the past two or three years? (2) How advanced is the congregation's understanding of biblical stewardship? (3) How many of the members currently use estimate-of-giving cards? (4) What is the per-capita giving of members? (5) Is the congregation planning any major appeals (such as a capital-fund drive) during the year? (6) What has *not* worked well in the past? Why?

After the type of appeal has been determined, careful attention to the nuts and bolts is essential. The following eight points are key.

1. Decide to make the appeal before building the budget. Congregations that prepare their budget before they conduct an appeal are putting the train in front of the engine. In what ways are people motivated to give money to good causes? People respond best when asked to give to people they trust. Second, they give to ministries in which they believe. Last and least, they give to paper—brochures, letters, budgets. Not only is the budget an ineffective vehicle for increasing giving, using the budget as a fund-raising tool will invariably hold down the level of giving.

2. Get the best people involved. Go after the best and only the best! The best people to lead a stewardship appeal may include members of the congregation who are not members of any committee. Every church has a cadre of special people who are distinguished as stewards. Some of these probably are already serving on the stewardship committee. Others may not be on any committee and would be happy to help for a few weeks. If it follows a year-round model, a stewardship committee will have enough to do throughout the year. It may, therefore, be a good idea to appoint a special task force to head up the appeal. If so, asking one or several members of the stewardship committee to serve with the task force will facilitate coordination.

Action Possibility: Early in the year, prepare a list of people who have served in stewardship capacities in the past. Add to that list each month the names of other people who would make effective stewardship leaders. These may include people who are practicing tithers and those who could make effective stewardship talks. Invite also other respected members of the congregation whose spiritual commitment qualifies them to serve.

3. Schedule events carefully. Stewardship does not happen in a vacuum. It is not enough for steering-committee members to be aware of their own specific responsibilities. Committee and task-force members must be alert to the way various elements of the program dovetail. How do the tasks of the committee chairperson interface with those of the financial secretary? How does the progression of stewardship talks fit together? Just as important, how does the appeal fit into the church calendar?

Action Possibility: Prepare copies of the Stewardship Appeal Calendar for every member of the stewardship committee and appeal task force. Make it specific. Include all dates, specific events, and especially, the names and phone numbers of the persons responsible. The chair can use this calendar to check each week with members to be sure everything is on schedule.

4. *Get people's attention.* Lyle Schaller once said that if you want a congregation to be aware of an event you are planning, tell the people five different times in five different ways. A key ingredient to effective stewardship programs is redundancy. *A key ingredient to effective stewardship programs is redundancy!*

Repetition of information will include multiple morning announcements and two or three separate mailings. Stewardship talks that build on each other, Sunday school announcements, and appropriate reference to the program in both adult and children's sermons can also help to strengthen the communication effectiveness.

5. *Say what you mean and mean what you say.* A guest leader for a stewardship appeal was asked, "When we invite people to church on commitment Sunday, should we tell them there will be an invitation to make an estimate of giving?"

That leader responded, "I don't think that's necessary. You get them there and I'll ask them."

But if there is a lack of clarity regarding the purpose of some parts of the appeal, some people may develop a perception of deception. Worse still, some leaders who feel a bit reluctant about asking people to give may intentionally keep the campaign so low in profile that members "see through a glass dimly." Low key can become no key. The committee members must not be the only persons aware of the events transpiring in the stewardship appeal. Every member of the congregation must know everything that is happening. If a person arrives on a commitment Sunday or at the beginning of a visitation program and does not know what is happening, it is imperative that the only acceptable explanation be that the person has been at the North Pole during the weeks prior to the campaign.

6. *Don't apologize.* A reluctant advocate was making a presentation about tithing and percentage giving in small-group sessions. Not a tither himself, he felt somewhat awkward inviting others to become tithers. After making his presentation, he came to the bottom line—the part where he was to ask the question:

"Folks, I have a request that I've been told to make at this point. I really hate to ask this. And I want you to know, if you don't feel comfortable with it, that's all right. I know it's hard, and a lot of you won't be able to do it. I wonder if some of you might consider . . . would some of you be willing to try tithing? Now, if you can't, I understand."

While others who were leading the same program found that 25 out of 35 participants agreed to grow toward and beyond tithing, only two or three responded to this man's appeal. (One wonders if they were already tithers.)

Apologizing for asking people to do ministry is like apologizing for the crucifixion. Our Lord does not want us to make apologies, but to repent of our sins and turn to God for newness of life. True repentance means to turn around. True repentance rouses us to minister in Christ's name. We do not apologize for being compelled by our love for God to give.

7. Attendance and participation are crucial. Presence and involvement of the members is a prime prediction of outcome and income. Stewardship traditionally has *not* been the most exciting ministry for a congregation. This is due in part to the bad press that stewardship often receives. Many leaders have labeled it as a necessary evil. Reversing people's opinions about stewardship programs is therefore one of the more important aspects of stewardship education and interpretation. The best stewardship program will fall flat if it does not involve the people in ways that allow the inspiration of the gospel to work in their hearts.

8. Tabulate the results. Many congregations go to considerable expense and effort to conduct an effective appeal, only to drop the ball with a weak "thank you" when it is over. Most published stewardship programs say little about tabulating the results. They assume that congregations will determine their total giving as a direct result of an appeal, but give no instructions for tabulating or reporting. Unfortunately, some stewardship leaders report the number of estimates that have been received and the amount reflected by the estimates, but end their report short of sharing a total expected income. Thus, to the members, an appeal that succeeded does not seem like a success.

Regardless of the type of annual appeal used, some people who give regularly will not fill out an estimate. Unless these members are assigned a figure for anticipated income to the church, based on their last year's giving record, the projection is not based on responsible figures.

Few people, except in special circumstances, will lower their giving. If they do not fill out an estimate of giving card, most will give the same amount as the previous year. A few will grow in their giving, realizing that it is a part of their Christian commitment. A step-by-step procedure for completing this tally is found in Appendix D.

Step Two: Prepare the Budget

The leaders of Fading Glory Church take great pride in the fact that they do not prepare a budget. Their motto is, "Whatever people give, that's what we'll spend." Congregations that use no budget or spending plan are in the minority today. While smaller congregations can probably "get along" without a budget, a budget will provide increased clarity for mission in even the smallest church.

For at least four reasons, every church can benefit from building a budget: (1) A budget is one means, among others, to *strategize for mission.* A properly prepared budget enables people to consider future goals and make plans to attain them. (2) A budget is a *tool for management;* it makes the management of the congregation's resources more effective. It allocates funds to the various ministries on a priority basis and enables proper checks and balances on indiscriminate spending. (3) A budget is an effective *tool for evaluation.* Current programs and ministries need to be evaluated annually on the basis of their effectiveness, their use of the financial resources allocated, and the objectives attained.

The various committees of the congregation should begin this process. They should be up front in asking the difficult questions about mission and ministry. Rather than designate the same amount to a function each year, inquire first whether this ministry is one in which they should be engaged. Questions might include: Is this a viable ministry for the coming year, or has it run its course? Or, does this ministry duplicate another we're already doing? Did this ministry begin as someone's pet project? Should this ministry be expanded? In the rare cases in which a ministry has fulfilled its purpose, the committee closest to the action should prune with vengeance. (4) A not unimportant purpose of the budget is to *authorize spending.*

Budgets are seen from two perspectives in most congregations. They may be a canon so rigidly cast in brass that they are more hindrance than help. Such congregations and governing boards benefit from loosening up a bit, since a budget policy of this type can inhibit ministry. It is better to view a budget as a guide for spending or a plan for ministry. Some congregations have begun calling them "spending plans" or "guides for spending," in order to reduce the inflexibility to which some leaders are prone.

On the other hand, the other extreme of paying no attention to budget figures is equally dangerous. Disregarding budget line items equals having no budget whatever. So procedures should be in place for making mid-year changes when they are necessary.

Budget preparation is one of those tasks that many finance or budget committees dread. An all-too-common scenario for budget preparation is to look at what was spent last year and "guestimate" what to add for next year. The committee then factors in inflation and how much it thinks might be needed if ministry is to be expanded. Such budgets are usually written with little creativity and presented with less. In these situations, members of the congregations usually regard the budget meeting as either a ho-hum experience or as a forum to raise concerns about single line items.

Creative congregations, however, view the budget process as an opportunity to tell their mission story in new and exciting ways. Each year, the budget presentation is anticipated as an imaginative and exhilarating look at our stewardship in action. They remember that:

- A budget is a tool. It should enhance conscientious management.
- A budget is a plan, an estimate, and a projection. Judgments that went into its preparation need to be reevaluated throughout the year.
- An effective budget needs to be flexible. It is only as accurate as it was on the day it was adopted. If new opportunities for ministry arise, new crises occur, or circumstances change, leaders must be able to adjust the budget.

The step-by-step process for preparing a budget that is actually the plan for ministry will vary with the type of budget being developed. The governing board of a congregation should determine which type will be most helpful in conveying the message of mission to the membership. While there are variations on these budget types, there are two basic approaches.

Creating a budget is more than completing a spreadsheet. The spreadsheet is the final step. Step one, as outlined above, is to determine what income the congregation can expect for the coming year. Once projections of income are in place, the appropriate committee can begin steps to prepare the plan for ministry.

The line-item budget is probably the most frequently used. This spreadsheet-type budget lists, line-by-line, the dollars spent on benevolence, salaries, utilities, insurance, mortgage payments, and program expenses.

71

The program budget offers an opportunity to promote creatively the ministry of the congregation, while at the same time providing a clear and concise overview of the costs. A program budget paints a vivid picture of ministry for members of the congregation. Technically, it is the budget stated in programmatic terms. Actually, it enables members to focus on mission and ministry. The program budget is a plan for growing in ministry. The program areas of the congregation are listed. These might include the six ministry areas of partnership, worship, learning, witness, service, and support. All costs required for programs that fall under these areas are listed with each program section.

With this approach, the viability of a specific program can be used to determine its effectiveness by comparing costs with mission accomplished. Items that cross more than one ministry area, such as the pastor's salary, are divided proportionately among the programs and ministries that include the pastor's participation. Expenses for office supplies and staff, including items often viewed as overhead for the ministry they support, are allocated to the programs affected. *True "overhead" does not exist in a mission-oriented congregation!* All expenses are a means of accomplishing its mission goals.

Many congregations write a line-item budget and then convert it to a program budget. The program budget, however, can also be constructed by establishing a need and setting goals. The format of the budget becomes a tool for planning, evaluation, and communication. Costs are clearly shown and detailed for all expenditures, but the focus is on the life and mission of the congregation.

Action Possibility: The foremost call of the church is to look beyond itself. Beginning budget preparation with the partnership ministries of the church avoids the "myopia trap." When conflict raged in Corinth, and the people there could not see beyond their own desperation, Paul urged them to look beyond their own needs to the needs of others. If a congregation truly sees its outreach to others as a primary call from God, placing the benevolence goals of the congregation first in the budget prevents "ministry beyond ourselves" from being relegated to the leftovers.

"Well, folks, it looks like the worst is out of the way," commented Dick, smiling impishly. "The appeal netted a handsome increase, and we've just about wrapped up the budget for another year. Time to put it to bed and wait for the congregational meeting, right?"

"Wrong!" shouted almost everyone in the room.

"And you know it, don't you?" Ann grinned. "I know you're about to pass the baton, but don't think for a moment that we haven't learned anything from you these past two years. We're just two-thirds of the way home. Now we need to decide the best way to share the story with the congregation."

"Right," replied Dick. "The congregation needs to know that we've heard their suggestions and requests, and we want to reflect their vision in the budget."

"What we need most is another creative way to present the total picture to our members," Jackie suggested. She had been listening quietly, amused at the goings on. "I loved what we did last year—and I think everyone else did too. When you illustrated the budget with slides, it came across powerfully. I couldn't imagine anyone not taking a great deal of satisfaction in what our church is doing for the Lord. I don't mean that we should be unduly proud, but I felt we communicated what the church is all about."

"It was a little time consuming, writing the script and getting pictures of all our ministries, but those of us who worked on it actually got so excited that we could hardly stop," Dick commented.

"How well I remember," Larry agreed. "We worked until three o'clock in the morning, weaving together the script, the dissolve unit, and the slides to make the presentation smooth. But it was worth every minute!"

"The most frequent comment I heard, after it was all

over," replied Ann, "was that people didn't realize how much our church is doing for our members and community and around the world."

"It was exciting," said Dick. "But now I think we're open to suggestions for this year."

"What's wrong with repeating the multimedia-type presentation?" asked Jackie. "It went over so big last year, I can't think people wouldn't appreciate another one just like it. Of course we'd change the script and the slides, but I think it would work well. Besides, now that we know what we're doing, it should be easier this year."

"I wouldn't argue against that," replied Ann, "but what are some of our other options? Maybe we should think about them before we lock into anything."

"I've never seen a more creative presentation than Larry made two years ago," noted Dick. "I realize the charts and graphs may not speak to everyone. But I thought that when he was finished, everyone had a refreshing look at our ministry.

"I've got another idea, though," he continued. "Last year our pictures moved very well on the screen because of the dissolve unit. We even managed to get a couple of zooming effects. So why not go another step this year and use a video production? We could use some actual candid shots, as well as some staged sections. And instead of just talking about ministry to homebounds, we could interview one of them.

"I even know a couple of members who are good with video equipment and know how to edit tape. Now that our program budget is in place, we could just follow it as an outline and move from one section to another. Our denomination has even put together some tape on our mission fields. Maybe they could provide some footage for a short segment on our missionary sponsorship."

"I didn't think we could improve much on last year," replied Ann, "but I think you just did!"

VI

THE NEED OF THE GIVER

Friends and admirers were backed up for almost a block at the beautiful old funeral home. People were standing three-deep in line waiting to pay their final respects to a man the whole town had come to love and admire. Some of those who stood in the four-inch-deep snow had never even met him. But he had touched their lives, and they felt compelled to pay tribute to one who had virtually become the father of the whole community.

During the long wait, people began to chat. The subject was always "Walter."

"I only met him once," commented a young woman shivering from the cold, "but he changed my life. You see, I came to this town with my husband and three kids. I hadn't been here three weeks until my husband took off and left me and the kids alone. Why, I was so scared I thought I'd die. I didn't have much education and hadn't planned to work until the kids were older. My neighbor heard about my problem, and she called Walter. He didn't even come over, but sent word that he had a job I could start the next week and a warm apartment that would be free until I could get on my feet. It was four months before I could even begin to pay rent.

"Two years later, I went to him to make arrangements for payments on the back rent, and you know what he said? He looked over the top of his reading glasses and said, 'Thank you, but I never intended you to pay for those months. You just go out there and find somebody in need, and help them.' So I did. I went straight to my pastor and asked if he could suggest somebody who needed help. And it felt so good to give instead of receive, I just kept on helping them. Walter taught me how good it feels to give."

The man standing behind her smiled and said, "That sounds just like ol' Walt. I'll bet that everyone standing in this line has the same kind of story to tell. I knew him for about twenty years, and I've gotta say that I've never known a more giving man."

An older man, perhaps in his seventies, turned around to face the couple.

"I couldn't help overhearing your story," he said. "We've all got 'em, that's for sure. Walt and I went to school together. We were best friends. We even joined the service together, but then we got separated. When the war was over, he didn't come home right away. I tried to trace him, but just when I was about to give up, he got off the bus one day, still wearing his uniform. He'd been a POW.

"He stood up in church one Sunday morning and asked if he could say a few words. The pastor never got to preach, and no one cared. He told what he'd been through, and how he'd come to realize that the only important thing in life was God, his family, and helping other people. From that day on, he lived the way he thought Christ would live, if the Lord had been born rich. He said he knew he could never do it, but he'd like to try to outgive God. He said giving was the best reason for living he'd come across."

Giving is the reason for living. In survey after survey, people say that their primary reason for giving is gratitude to God for the blessings they have received. Christian people, from new-born believers to mature disciples, seem to realize that giving is intrinsic to being a Christian.

Why People Give

In a cartoon, the officiating clergyman says, "I would like to remind you that what you are about to give is deductible, cannot be taken with you, and is considered by some to be the root of all evil."

Leaders of congregations need to take heed lest such comic examples be acted out in real life. People do not give because they gain a tax deduction. They do not give because they know they cannot take it with them. They do not give because they think money is the root of all evil. But people do like to give for at least seven positive reasons:

1. Giving is a grateful response to God. Gratitude for all the blessings God has given is the number-one reason people give. Christian people have a built-in desire to say thank you. They like to give because they have already received. Giving is thus an act of worship, as well as an act of thanksgiving. They give as a response to God's giving.

Several children were being asked why they gave to their church. They came up with different reasons, all of which were good.

Finally, one little girl, about nine years old, said, "Well, when you give, you give to God." For her, that was the bottom line. That is also the strongest motive for giving in the minds of adults.

2. Giving adds meaning to life. There is nothing bad about feeling good, especially when the good feeling accompanies acts that follow the example of Christ. Giving adds meaning to our lives. Giving is one of the primary joys of living.

In Victor Hugo's great novel *Les Miserables*, Jean Valjean is befriended and given lodging by a bishop. He then returns the bishop's kindness by stealing his candlesticks. The police bring Jean back to the bishop's home for questioning, and when it appears that Jean is headed for jail, the bishop offers a plausible explanation for the missing candlesticks. Jean Valjean is amazed.

When the two are alone, Jean asks, "Why did you do that? You know I am guilty."

The bishop replies, "Life is for giving."

3. People like to help people. Thanksgiving Day spelled tragedy for one family in a small town. A raging fire broke out in their home while they were visiting relatives, and the family returned to find that almost everything they had was lost. The community rallied to help them. Some neighbors provided a place for them to stay until they could rent a home. Others brought clothing, food, and furniture. On Sunday morning, the pastors of the town asked for a special offering to help the besieged family, and thousands of dollars poured in. Christian people are generous. They want to give to help other people. Churches with high levels of giving therefore tend to say strongly and often, "Our church is helping people. Thanks for making that possible."

Action Possibility: Point to the people dimension. When presenting members with an opportunity to support a ministry, be sure to illustrate how this will have an impact on people.

4. People know that giving their money is a spiritual response to God's gift of our salvation. John Wesley said, "If people were more alive to God, they would be more liberal." Giving liberally is a direct consequence of commitment to Christ. Christian stewardship is a spiritual matter. The writer of First John declares, "We love because [Christ] first loved us" (4:19). We know how to express Christian love because we have first experienced the sacrificial giving love of Jesus Christ. In the same way, we give because Christ first gave to us. As love begets love, so giving begets giving. The offering is one more way to express our appreciation to God for the greatest gift of all—the gift of our redemption.

Action Possibilities:
- To assist people in understanding the offering as an act of worship, receive the offering in different ways. Invite people to bring their offering to the altar area of the church as an added expression of their gratitude to God. Remind them that part of every offering is a thank offering to God.
- At what point in the worship service is the offering scheduled? In some congregations, it is received early, to "get it out of the way." Other churches place the offering at a point where its very location reminds people that their giving is a response to all that God has done. Having the offering following the reading and preaching of the Word may help to remind people that giving, too, is a response to God's grace.

5. *Someone asks them to give.* One congregation that had just begun its building program decided to conduct an every-member appeal. The committee felt the need for assistance in such a great undertaking, so they hired a firm that specialized in capital-fund drives for churches. Following the firm's advice, they listed the names of members they thought would be able to make substantial contributions. Their program director reminded them that few people are offended when asked for more than they are able to give, so they decided to ask each major donor for a specific amount.

They were elated when one man made the requested gift of $50,000 without batting an eye. A few weeks later, that man also made a donation of $1 million to a special community cause. Over lunch with his pastor, he asked how the campaign was going.

During the discussion, he commented, "You know, I was delighted to give the $50,000 you requested. But with such a major appeal, I was surprised that you didn't ask for more."

Most people have a strong internally programmed desire to say yes when someone asks them to give. But another part of their internal software is equally dependable. People almost never give beyond what is requested. Churches that ask for too little from their members will get what they ask for. When congregations invite their members to grow in their giving, most members will stretch themselves to meet the challenge.

6. People give to people they trust. Who is asking for the money is often as important in obtaining a positive response as the purpose for the money. The most effective stewardship is relational—not functional or organizational or institutional. People give confidently to people they see as worthy, just as they give to causes they believe are worthy. Stewardship must therefore be built on the relationships of respect, trust, and integrity which are already solidly in place in the congregation.

Action Possibility: When making financial requests to the congregation, invite respected church members to make the appeal. This is helpful during special appeals, advance gifts, and major gifts (though the latter usually should be requested in person). Do not rely only on those who are members of the finance or stewardship committee, or even on the church's governing body. Members who are respected by other members and are known for their integrity have a special built-in ability to request gifts. Nor should pastors assume that because members expect them to ask, they are therefore a poor choice as the person to make a request. In some cases, the pastor may well be the best person.

7. People believe in the mission or ministry to which they give. People give to their church because they believe in its mission. Conversely, people will not give to anything in which they do not believe. We can provide an excellent reason for giving by stressing the mission we intend to accomplish in service of our Lord. In the Corinthian letters, Paul lifted up a ministry with which everyone could agree. The hungry and the oppressed bring tears to almost every eye. The church also has a built-in given. People love their church and tend to believe strongly in its mission. That pull becomes especially powerful when the church vividly illustrates the worthy needs they will help to meet.

Stewardship Versus Fund-raising

Churches with high levels of giving accent the need of the giver to give, rather than the need of the congregation to receive. Emphasizing the need of the giver places stewardship in a spiritual realm. Stressing the need of the congregation to receive places stewardship in the arena of fund-raising.

Stewardship and fund-raising are often confused in church life. There is a basic difference between the two. Good stewardship raises funds, but good stewardship does not stop with fund-raising. Fund-raising is a matter of putting together enough money to pay an organization's bills. Fund-raising is raising enough money to balance a budget. Fund-raising is asking people to fill up the thermometer on the United Way chart. Fund-raising helps many organizations accomplish some important goals. Churches that try to finance their ministries through fund-raising techniques, however, consign themselves to eternally mediocre results.

While fund-raising is a financial matter, stewardship is a spiritual matter. Stewardship relates to the way we live out our commitment to Jesus Christ. Talk about money has developed a bad reputation in many congregations. One reason is that the leaders too often focus their energies on trying to raise money, rather than on trying to raise the spiritual level of their members. And the gimmicky tricks dreamed up in this misdirected focus often backfire.

Fund-raising is not, however, a dirty word. It does good and is important to the well-being of our society. According to the American Association of Fund-Raising Counsel Trust for Philanthropy (1991), charitable giving reached $122 billion in 1990. Eighty-four percent of that money came from individuals who responded to fund-raising efforts of organizations and institutions. The vast majority went to causes that nearly everyone would list as "good and important."

Most of those gifts would not have been given, were it not for fund-raising. Organizations like the United Way are positive community-service organizations. They put their budgets together and then find the money to support them. In their kind of work, that is probably the best way to accomplish their goals. But too many sincere church leaders try to imitate that fund-raising technique in their churches.

Congregations that experience significant growth in stewardship do exactly the reverse. They do not raise money by asking, "How much money does the church need?" They know that this is the wrong question, because it is a fund-raising question. The spiritual question is, "How much money does God ask from me as a spiritual response of faith?" Paul counsels that we are to give as we have prospered. Nowhere in the New Testament are we told that we should give just to pay the church bills. Churches that reverse this emphasis are putting a lid on both their total income and the spiritual growth of their members.

While fund-raising techniques should not replace biblical stewardship, neither should the congregation's budget be used as the crux of the appeal. Setting the budget first puts us into a situation that might be called the gravy-bowl syndrome. If you grow up in a large family and there is a roast, potatoes, and a big bowl of gravy for dinner, you know how much of that gravy is yours. No one has to measure it out; each person around the table knows how much is his or her fair share.

The same is true of a church budget. The "gravy bowl" system builds the church budget first, then tries to raise enough money to pay the bills. A church that continually stresses the need of the church to receive, rather than the need of the giver to give, will hold down the level of giving. This dues-paying mentality produces more red ink than black ink on the church treasurer's report. But even more detrimental is the fact that the church is thereby blocking people from hearing the really important spiritual message inherent in stewardship. The question is never, "What does the church need to receive?" but rather, "What does God call me to give?"[10]

The Desire to Designate

"Tell us where our money is going. That's what we need to hear," commented a distracter at a cottage meeting. "All you've been talking about is how important it is for Christians to give. That's true, but people want to know where their money is going."

The distracter is not all wrong. There does seem to be a growing penchant for American Christians to wish to know more specifics regarding what their money is doing. And yes, churches do owe accountability to people for how they use the Lord's gifts. Also, wanting to know has a positive side effect: People are interested in the mission and ministry of their church. Stewardship interpretation helps people know and understand the causes, ministries, and programs to which they are asked to give. The more people know, the more they are inclined to give.

In the 1940s, financial needs of congregations and denominations increased dramatically. Churches found themselves conducting ever-more special appeals and offerings. Within a few years, church leaders discovered that members were feeling badgered and battered by all the special requests. To counter this trend, the concept of the unified budget developed. People could now make one single gift to their congregation, which covered all its ministries. The unified budget found strong support and is still used by many congregations.

By the mid-1960s, however, some leaders began to question the value of the unified budget. Congregations and church bodies were no longer able to fund their growing ministries. More denominational and congregational special appeals were being used. People began to argue that giving to the "pot" lacked a sense of belonging, of being a part of the ministry. Attitudes also changed. The trust of churches and leaders that earlier had been a natural part of society began to erode. People expected to take part in the decision-making process. Then too, after a number of years of unified budgets, some churches stopped doing the good "PR" work that they had done in earlier years. Lack of information began to cool peoples' excitement about ministry.

Other leaders still adamantly defended the unified budget on theological grounds. Special appeals seemed to suggest that the need of the church to receive was more important than the need of the giver to give. They also liked the simplicity of the unified budget approach, as well as the control it gave them. A considerable number of people have, however, continued to rebel against the unified approach, in favor of designating. Donations to causes outside the unified budget (and often even outside the church) have created a tension between church leaders and donors. It has often erected a we-they mentality that is unhealthy in Christian circles.

A Vital Balance

Stressing the need of the giver to give is not automatically a contradiction to designated giving. Today, it is more apparent that there needs to be a balance. Giving to ministry in general and the desire of members to designate special causes will work together if some simple factors are kept in mind. This is one area in which churches and members should be able to have their cake and eat it too.

84

High designated benevolence results in higher giving. Congregations that have a high level of support for designated benevolence tend to be above average in other measures of stewardship performance. How can we determine which is the chicken and which is the egg? Does high designated benevolence result in good giving, or does good giving directly affect designated benevolence? While both are true, it would seem that higher designated giving is more often the chicken—the prime mover. At least four possible reasons stand behind this pattern:

- Interest in special causes is an expression of congregational vitality often associated with good stewardship performance.
- Interest in special causes motivates members to give because of the personal or popular appeal that such causes often have.
- Giving for special causes is usually over and above previously established giving patterns.
- After support for special causes has begun, it tends to be continued. In most cases, congregations and their members seem to see this as a continuing commitment.[11]

Times of great need teach the need to give. Name a disaster almost anywhere in the world, and one can name a time when Christian people flock to the aid of other people. Hurricanes, earthquakes, floods, tornadoes—all bring out the best in Christian people. Every pastor can relate a time when a disaster brought a congregation to new levels of love and generosity. While all disasters are tragic, it is more devastating if Christians fail to respond to them and learn from them. They provide the opportunity to proclaim the need of the giver to give.

Sharing mission stories teaches the need to give. One of the negatives that often accompanied the use of a unified budget was a gradual decline by some congregations in telling the story of mission. This was certainly unintentional.

Nonetheless, failure to share mission stories with congregations reduces visibility and ultimately the desire to give. There are two sides to every "giving coin." On the one side is the need of the ministry for support; on the other is the need of the giver to give. Both are important. Stressing the need of the giver to give does not nullify the responsibility to keep people informed.

Tell them! A Sunday school teacher asked, "How can we help our people understand that the offering is an act of worship in the church?" Several good comments were made.

One person responded, "Invite people to bring their offering forward to the altar area occasionally."

Another commented, "Yes, there is no sacred way to receive an offering, as long as people understand that the church receives it on behalf of God."

Finally, one woman spoke up. "Well, tell us!" she demanded, and went on to say, "People just need to hear now and then that part of our worship is to give."

The same can be said for emphasizing the need of the giver to give. We simply need to say it. Christian people need to give. It is part and parcel of being a Christian.

Children's sermons teach the need to give. Stories such as *Ragman*[12] and *The Dance of the Heart*,[13] which teach children about the examples of others, help them to understand the need to give. The old proverb, "Train children in the way they should go, and when they are old, they will not depart from it" is true for stewardship too.

Pastor Dave sat in his office on Monday morning, giving considerable thought to the third in a series of stewardship sermons. The emphasis of the series had been on the need of the giver to fulfill Christ's mandate to serve. He sat, idly wondering if perhaps a third sermon in as many weeks on the need of the giver to give might be overkill.

Suddenly his intercom jarred him from his concentration.

"Karen is on line one," his secretary announced. Pastor Dave picked up the phone.

"I hope I'm not interrupting anything too important," Karen said, "but I couldn't resist calling this morning to say how much your sermon yesterday helped me. Ted and I talked about it all through lunch. We've always known that as Christians we give in response to God's love. We've even tried to grow in our giving each year, but something else you said about the practice of tithing was new to us both."

"Oh, what was that?" asked the pastor, feeling a bit more cheery than blue Mondays usually allow.

"It was right after you talked about the need to give a percent or a tithe of our income to the Lord. Then you said, 'If you're not sure what percent you're giving now, why not figure it out. Then consider growing by one percent next year? Better still, why not take the leap of faith, and move to a tithe, or beyond?'"

"Is that what moved you?" asked Dave.

"No, it was what came next. You then said, 'It is far easier for Christians to *act* our way into a new way of *thinking* than it is to *think* our way into a new way of *acting*.' That blew my mind at first, but I wrote it down so I wouldn't forget about it. At lunch, I commented to Ted that I always thought it was the other way around. We've always been taught that good theology and biblical understanding lead to good actions. But you seemed to be saying that the other way works too."

"That's right, Karen. Our church does believe in the value of correct biblical interpretation. But if our actions are sound, they too can lead us to new levels of biblical awareness. I think that when it comes to Christian giving, our actions often will lead us to better understanding and commitment. A step of faith is worth a thousand thoughts.

"For example, some people commit themselves to Christ, and then as a part of that commitment, start to tithe. Often they even find that, for them, tithing becomes a *minimum* standard for giving; many grow beyond the tithe. This principle comes through in the Scriptures, too—we are told to imitate Christ. Doing what Jesus did often leads us to think as Jesus thought."

"During lunch, Ted pointed out that this idea carries over into our secular lives too. He said that when he went through basic training in the army, one of the things they pounded into the heads of every recruit was, 'Act, don't think! When an order is given, you obey it; you don't analyze it.' Acting on an order in combat can save your life. If you stop to think, you might not be able to act."

"Karen, I have to admit that the idea takes a little getting used to for some of us. But I honestly believe that if more Christians would act out their faith as an imitation of Christ, their faith would grow too."

---VII---

VARIETY LEADS TO VITALITY

"I feel a bit like a lame duck in this meeting, since I'm going off the committee in a couple of months," Ed commented. "But this is a good time to take a look at where we've been and share some guidance for the coming year with your new chair. So, let's evaluate!"

Martha, who had come onto the committee in September to fill a vacancy, responded, "Well, I must admit that I didn't think serving on the stewardship committee when we were about to begin our fall appeal was a very good idea. But I have to tell you, I think I've learned more about stewardship in the last two months than in the last ten years."

"That's great to hear," replied Ed. "I felt a little guilty for asking when we were entering one of our busier seasons. However, when Paula moved away, she left a void that needed to be filled as quickly as possible."

"I'm sad that she moved, but I wouldn't trade the last two months for anything. It's not that stewardship was unfamiliar to me. I guess I'd always thought about it more from the perspective of esoteric Bible studies. Although those are important, I'm glad to get some new ideas about applying the Scriptures to my daily stewardship. I know we've done this same program for three years running. It was fun from the pew, and it was even better from backstage. Can we do it again next year?"

Jack, a local businessman, spoke up. "It's time for lesson two, Martha. One of the things we learned from our stewardship studies at the beginning of our meetings is that three successive years with any one program is 'max.' We may come back to it in a year or so, but we need a change for next year. Our next decision has to be, What do we do next? Right, Ed?"

"Right, Jack. Maybe since you're our new chairperson for next year, you should take over the evaluation."

"You're doing fine. My time will come. Besides, I'm not bashful. I'll interject my thoughts as we go."

"Very well. I've asked our financial secretary to join us tonight and share some facts and figures that might help us in planning for next year. Don, were you able to gather the figures I asked for?"

"Sure. All I had to do was go to our database, key in a few codes, and there it was. Aren't computers wonderful—most of the time?"

"I asked Don to bring us some information so that we can see how effective we've actually been. It's one thing to get the estimates from people, but if the money doesn't come in, that's another matter."

"You asked for the comparisons for the last three years. Last year, we received . . . well, let me just share in percentages. That'll make more sense than the actual dollars. Last year our pledged increase above the previous year was 22.4 percent, and we received 22.6 percent—over 100 percent! Two years ago, the congregation pledged an increase of 19.8 percent, and we actually received 20.1 percent over the previous year. Three years ago, our increase wasn't quite so good. We did have an increase in pledges of 18.3 percent, but the actual receipts indicate that we received 17.9 percent. Close, but not a bull's-eye.

"After checking that and thinking we were doing pretty

well, I went back one more year. The results were not so good four years ago. The pledged increase was only 12.3 percent, but the actual receipts indicate only a 10.4 percent increase. That's only about 82 percent of the pledged amount. Experts indicate that if we receive less than 92 to 95 percent, something is amiss."

Ruth spoke up. "What kind of follow-up did we do that year? We've been making a concerted effort these past three years to keep the congregation better informed, and it seems to have paid off. I wasn't on the committee three years ago. Was anything done in the way of follow-up?"

"Not much," replied Ed. "In fact, that was my first year on the committee, and that was our one big concern in our evaluation. The following year we made up for lost time. I don't think anyone thought we overdid it. We got a lot of positive feedback that said members appreciated our keeping them better informed. Thanks, Don, for giving us those figures."

Ed finished a couple of notes in his loose-leaf binder to pass along to Jack.

"It looks like we're on the right track. Now for the hard part. We can't repeat the same program again next year, so what shall we do? We don't need to make a decision at this meeting. But I'd suggest that by the January or February meeting, we know the program approach we intend to use."

Staying with the same annual stewardship appeal for more than three consecutive years nearly always results in the law of diminishing returns. At least three factors contribute to this decline in effectiveness: (1) *Leaders will be tempted to take more shortcuts with each successive year.* Doing surgery on stewardship programs tends to accidentally remove vital organs rather than fix those that are damaged. (2) *Variety leads to vitality.* If members were forced to listen to the same sermon week after week, it would become like stale bread. When people take the same route to work every day, they seldom stop to view the scenery. Stewardship programs and approaches need variety to keep from becoming moldy.

(3) *Stewardship, like all other facets of ministry, needs to be fun.*
People who love their work make better workers. When a
stewardship program retains its sparkle, it will most likely be
a successful appeal.

When it becomes tarnished from overexposure, it will
become "ho-hum." The mere fact that a program is fun,
however,is not a reason to keep it forever without a break.
One pastor related that his congregation became virtually
addicted to one campaign and would hear of no other for
more than eight years.

"We're in a rut," he said. "What's worse is that it's been so
much fun that my people don't even care."

An old Navajo sat by his campfire, responding to the
questions of his avid admirers. They were asking about his
life-style and traditions. In his stoic manner, he responded
thoroughly to each query. After a time the conversation
turned to bows and arrows and arrowheads.

After listening intently to the questions of a budding
young archer, the old man responded, "Any bow is a good
bow. The arrow is heap much work!"

When it comes to stewardship programs, almost any well-
designed program is a good program. But the arrows that
incite ministry by touching the hearts of our members
require "heap much work." The gravest mistake that congregations make involving stewardship appeals is inattention to
detail. The angles and points of any stewardship program
will make it or break it.

John was not a lazy pastor. In fact, the people of Christ
Church often asked him to slow down a bit. His people
trusted him and he trusted them. But John did find that he
had one weakness. It showed up last year during the annual
stewardship campaign. He set out in his usual fastidious
manner to organize and structure the program.

With the help of the stewardship committee, he had lined
up one of the best stewardship programs available. Someone
suggested the name of a person who was well equipped to

serve as chairperson of the appeal's steering committee. Her leadership skills were excellent. Her understanding of the principles of stewardship made her the first choice for the position. When asked, she agreed enthusiastically.

During the first meeting of the committee, the pastor and chairperson pointed out to everyone all the details that would need attention if the program were to be successful. From that time on, however, things went downhill. Both the pastor and chairperson had personal problems which took some of their attention from the program. The pastor had a brief illness, and the chairperson found that an ill family member demanded considerable attention during the weeks of the program. Consequently, neither did an adequate job of follow-up with other committee members.

The church did receive an increase, but it was far below that which could have been expected from an effectively run program. What began as a carefully planned and potentially successful program ended with a whimper.

In analyzing the program, John noted that he had simply relaxed too much after a good beginning. He trusted his chairperson, who deserved that trust. But he had failed to recognize that even the best of leaders may lapse a bit when a family crisis occurs. He now realized, too late, that he should have followed up with the chairperson and committee members during the second week of the program. Had he done so, many of the pitfalls could have been avoided. It was a negative lesson, but a mistake John vowed not to make again.

Reports like this are more common than uncommon. These experiences can be avoided by careful adherence to the details in a well-designed appeal.

Action Possibility: Develop a long-range plan for stewardship appeals. Create a list of three or four effective stewardship campaigns to be kept in the hopper. After one, two, or three years, with appropriate evaluation each year, move on to the next program. No rotation is sacred. It may even be that a favorite program could be alternated with the other two or three so that it is repeated more often. The following section lists some of the strengths and challenges inherent in various kinds of appeals. Notes for this chapter include additional information on where to obtain some of the better ones.

Strengths and Challenges

The old Navajo's saying—"Any bow is a good bow. The arrow is heap much work"—is true for most stewardship appeals. However, some stewardship appeals are more effective than others for certain congregational circumstances. A capital-fund drive will benefit from a professionally led Every Member Visit. A congregation that has just conducted a capital drive may want to use a program that is more low-key, since the groundwork has already been laid. Every program has its strengths and its challenges. A challenge becomes a weakness only if it is disregarded. Properly addressed during the appeal, challenges can be turned into strengths.

Space limitations prevent a listing of every type of campaign available, but here are several useful campaigns, along with their strengths and challenges.

Consecration Sunday—This program focuses on a Sunday when every member of the congregation is invited to an inspirational worship service, at which estimates of giving are presented. Members then share a catered luncheon at which totals are announced and a celebration occurs. An outside guest leader is recruited to lead these events. The main energies of the congregation are directed toward promoting a high attendance for Consecration Sunday. During the month before Consecration Sunday, both the mail and stewardship talks are used to emphasize a biblical understanding for stewardship and anchor the date firmly in members' minds. Congregations that use this method often report a 15 to 30 percent increase in income over the previous year.[14]

Strengths
- Little time or training necessary for committee or participants.
- Materials can be easily distributed.
- Low cost for program, mailings, luncheon.
- Allows for one effective presentation and avoids risking mixed messages through different approaches by leaders.
- Use of a guest leader is a must and a plus.
- Personal visitation required only to receive reservations for the luncheon.
- Involves a spirit of celebration along with the realization that stewardship can be fun.

Challenges
- A poor choice of guest leader can affect the results.
- Little chance for dialogue except at the luncheon.
- Reaches homebound and those not in attendance only after the celebration is over.
- Will not reach "uncommitted" members (but then, what appeal does?).

Cottage Visits—These "Home Stewardship Meetings" attempt to enlist each family to attend a meeting in another member's home. At each meeting, a carefully trained team of leaders makes a presentation. (Audiovisual presentations may also be used, so that all are consistent.) Discussion follows. Often the small-group meetings are either held simultaneously or within a week, to emphasize the importance of the appeal. Estimates of giving may be received in the small groups, although this is sometimes reserved for a later worship service.

Strengths
- Allows for dialogue.
- Can organize members according to geographical areas, interest, or time available.

- Strengthens fellowship.
- Creates a high level of interest.
- Good education tool.
- Can make good use of audiovisuals.

Challenges
- Time consuming.
- Needs telephone callers to remind people to attend.
- Reservations are an absolute "must" to ensure reasonably good attendance.
- Training required for the presenters and discussion leaders.
- Careful organization needed so details essential to the success of the program cannot be overlooked.
- Does not reach less committed members.
- More difficult in larger congregations.
- Negative voices can dominate in group discussions.
- Reaches only those who attend meetings.
- Requires extensive follow-up.

Every-Member Visits—This involves personal visits with all members of the congregation in their homes. It requires training visitors to make careful presentations on congregational dreams and goals, and on Christian stewardship. Since each team of callers is expected to make only five or six visits, extensive recruiting of visitors is required. Commitments should be received by the callers in sealed envelopes. Professional visitation directors are available to assist congregations in conducting Every-Member Visitations.[15]

Strengths
- Carefully outlined manuals are available from many denominational stewardship offices.
- Includes all church members (except nonresidents and totally inactive members).

- Face-to-face discussion allows for questions, answers, and feedback.
- Allows visitors to share the congregation's vision for ministry rather than merely request commitments.
- Over time, permits personal growth and acceptance of pledging.
- A good starting point for stewardship education in the weeks prior to the visit.
- Involves the whole congregation.
- Helps update membership rolls.
- Follow-up usually is included and is necessary.

Challenges
- Requires a great deal of time, leadership, and training; takes up to three months, and as much as one-fourth of the congregation to make visits.
- Often difficult to recruit enough visitors.
- Follow-up is difficult to complete, but essential.
- Calls are sometimes interpreted as only asking for money rather than being interested in hearing member's needs.
- The budget should *not* be used.

Direct-Mail Campaign—This is designed to provide a low-key type of program. It may serve well in cases where there has been an adequate emphasis due to a special campaign such as a capital-fund drive. Direct-mail campaigns tend to reach people through inspiration, more than through a biblical/theological approach.[16]

Strengths
- Provides a low-key approach when and if that is desired due to other stewardship emphases.
- Letters are well written.
- Program is easy to conduct.

Challenges
- A low-key approach is often not the best way to teach sound biblical stewardship.
- May need to be supplemented with some biblical material or stewardship talks.
- Materials can be costly.
- Failure to follow the program as written in order to save some costs will often result in considerably lower returns.

Personal Delivery Systems—These have several names: *Circuit Rider,*[17] *Pony Express,*[18] *Up and Running,*[19] and others. They involve organizing the congregation into several chains, or trails, of families. The first family is to call on the second and deliver a packet of materials, including commitment cards. The second family is to call on the third, and so on, until all have been contacted. The signed and sealed pledge cards usually are placed in the packet. In some cases they may be presented at a later worship service.

Strengths
- Cuts down on travel time.
- Little training needed.
- Highlights confidentiality.
- Involves a large number of people in a nonthreatening way.
- Little time required.
- Is fun, often stimulating a creative, playful spirit.

Challenges
- Can encounter delays and breakdowns in delivery system.
- The process can become more important than the objective.
- Difficult for homebounds to participate.
- Need training for "trail bosses," or team leaders.

- Little dialogue about the mission of the congregation.
- Little or no opportunity for stewardship education.

Faith Promise Plan—This plan stresses the divine-human dimension of Christian commitment, rather than loyalty to the church or its mission. Like other effective appeals, it stresses the need of the giver to give rather than the need of the church to receive. Members are not asked to submit pledges or estimates of giving. Instead, they are asked to make a "faith promise" of the amount they will strive to give as the Lord blesses their lives. The faith promise should also include the percentage of their income. As a separate act of commitment, members are asked to provide a card indicating that they have submitted a faith promise. With this information, the committee is able to follow up on those who did not make a commitment.

Strengths
- Saves time, money, and planning.
- Appeals to the "best" in members.
- Can have a strong biblical motivation.
- May help some congregations grow toward pledging when it has not been a part of their tradition.
- Assures confidentiality.
- Can be used for special offerings.
- Appeals to more "conservative" congregations.

Challenges
- Reaches only highly committed members.
- Difficult for congregation to set goals and budget based on commitments, since a final tally may not be as accurate.
- Relies on clergy for motivation.
- May encourage a temptation to misuse the Bible, proof-texting, literalism, etc.
- Can encourage a step away from responsible pledging.

Appeal Follow-up

A group of pastors in an ecumenical ministerial association were discussing their various stewardship appeals. After several more experienced pastors had alluded to their programs, Al, a young seminary graduate beginning ministry in his first congregation raised a concern:

"In my congregation, the financial secretary reports every month how far we're behind on our pledges. The governing board has had some serious questions about whether to even ask for pledges, since actual income is often 8 to 12 percent below what is pledged. I'd sure appreciate some advice from the rest of you about how I might deal with this."

One pastor commented, "I found that to be a difficulty the first year or so that we had estimates of giving. People were a little confused as to what should be included. Once they understood it better, we got at least 95 percent each year."

Two of the older pastors remarked that they had had similar problems. One commented that in a congregation he had served, giving actually outstripped the estimates, while in another, the best he could get was about 95 percent of estimated income.

He went on, "I think one of the biggest reasons for the differences was in the way the churches did the follow-up after the appeal was over. In the church where more than 100 percent came in, we made certain to do some kind of follow-up each month. In fact, follow-up procedures were written out in detail in the committee agenda, so that it wouldn't be overlooked. Different approaches were taken each month, with different people actually doing the reporting. Rarely did the report merely consist of someone making an announcement.

"We tried to be creative. On one occasion near the beginning of summer, a farmer dressed in overalls came charging down the isle. He then entered into a dialog skit with the pastor. Of course, the newsletter always contained some kind of report, but the format was changed from month to month. We always liked to think that the appeal is really not over until the year is over. The gathering of estimates is only one part of the appeal. Follow-up is essential."

A fourth pastor spoke up. "I was in a congregation one time that was fraught with feuding. Some of the members used their giving as a way of voting for or against others in leadership capacities. It took me several years to deal with the conflict, but when harmony finally was restored, we received 95 to 98 percent of our committed dollars each year. It seemed to be a question of maturity. There were no easy answers, and the problem took several years to overcome."

"I've never experienced that," commented another younger pastor, "but I guess I've been lucky. I do know a classmate who had that problem, though. In his congregation it seemed to be directly related to the turnover in membership. He was near a military base, and he found that he lost as much as 30 percent of his members each year. To address the concern, he made certain that new-member classes helped people to see the relation between turnover and giving. He found that the members often did better after that, in part because they understood the problem."

Occasionally, congregations report that they conclude what appears to be an excellent appeal, with measurable results, only to find that the money simply does not appear. While there is *no cure-all* for such a problem, there are some strategies that may help when congregations receive less than 92 to 95 percent of the amount of committed dollars.

Follow-up should take different forms.

1. Begin your commitment period immediately following the appeal, rather than waiting until the beginning of a new fiscal year.

2. Send quarterly reports year-round, rather than waiting until late in the year. These are usually well worth the postage.

3. Be sure to follow up immediately after the campaign by

contacting members who have not participated in the program.

4. Use your church newsletter to communicate where the congregation is in relation to receipts versus commitments.

5. Do not hesitate at some point during the year to send out a pastoral letter encouraging members to check the amount of their giving in relation to their commitment.

6. An announcement on a Sunday at the end of the quarter, indicating the percentage of committed dollars received, may be helpful.

7. Stress year-round stewardship, emphasizing that stewardship is our whole ministry.

8. Remember that communication and information are foundational to participation.

"Let's not forget one very important thing," said Jack. "All these nuts and bolts programs that we do are crucial to our congregation, but—"

"Yes, Jack, that much I've learned," Martha interrupted. "The most important ingredient in any program is the people with whom we minister. Stewardship programs have only one purpose: to enhance people's awareness that being a gospel-oriented church is doing faithful stewardship."

"If stewardship is not presented as a part of our spiritual commitment to Jesus Christ, we will have failed," responded Ed. "Program approaches are important, but they must always be seen as the means to an end. The end is spiritual as well as financial growth."

"To be a mature Christian means to be a good steward. Being a poor steward might call into question one's spiritual maturity," Don reflected. "The call of Christ on our lives is the call to stewardship. Yes, there are many different aspects of stewardship, but one of these certainly has to be financial."

"I think you're making a really important point," interjected the pastor. "The basic nature of sin is not pride, as many theologians have defined it, but rather sloth or selfishness, pursuing our own interests first. It's sort of 'seeking our kingdom first,' instead of God's kingdom. Mature Christians will not take personal possessions more seriously than they take God. They know that possessions are temporary, sort of on-loan from God. And a mature disciple will have a sense of understanding about giving to an imperfect institution. After all, our gift is really to God, not to a less-than-perfect organization."

"Thanks, folks," laughed Jack. "I knew my point wouldn't fall on deaf ears in this bunch. Our goal in stewardship development is always first and foremost, spiritual growth!"

VIII

THE MORE THE MERRIER (MOST OF THE TIME)

"Exhaustion! That's what I feel right now. I'm so exhausted that I think if I even hear the word *stewardship* in the next month, I'll lose it."

Edna had just finished leading the annual stewardship appeal in her congregation. Her comment was made to the pastor and Mark, the one other person who had been enlisted to assist with the program. Mark had been called out of town on a family emergency for two weeks, so Edna had ended up doing many of the things Mark would have done.

Edna's first mistake was that she made a wrong assumption. She sincerely believed that most church members think of *stewardship* as "the S word." She was afraid people would be unwilling to help in the task. Since she personally felt rejected when people said, "No," she just never got around to asking anyone else to help.

Edna also found a considerable difference between her own leadership style and that of the pastor. The pastor was a laissez-faire leader. He felt that his role was to find the best person for a job, and then let that person "have at it."

During the stewardship program, he had stepped into the

background, saying that if Edna needed help to be sure to call. Edna's style of leadership was very hands-on. Had she had a sufficient number of people to help, all would have gone well. As it was, when she first looked at the task, she had believed it too large for two people to handle. Rather than enlist more help, she abbreviated some elements of the program. Others, she eliminated. But the task was still too much for one, so she overloaded herself. The result: burnout!

If there are not enough people to make a task manageable, even the most important and inspiring ministries can boil to burnout. Many congregations complain that 80 percent of the work is done by 20 percent of the people. When it comes to stewardship programs, that formula is often an understatement. Questions abound in governing-board meetings about how to involve more people in the process. The 20 percent (or less) are in danger. Worse yet, when one person runs hither and yon like the proverbial chicken, the fires that lead to burnout get hotter.

Yes, a few of the 80 percent are people who have already burned out. But most of the 80 percent are more in danger of rusting out from disuse. Enlisting their support will take creative recruitment, but for their spiritual benefit as well as for the protection of the minority, expanding the base is essential.

Dynamics of a Creative Leadership

Four common "threads of gold" can help congregational leaders reduce the levels of both burnout and rust out.

1. Creative Recruitment. "I'd like to call your attention to a couple of announcements in the bulletin," remarked Pastor Dan. "First, the meeting of the Women's Aid Executive Committee on Tuesday night. Hope you can come. Next, please note the invitation to anyone interested in serving on the stewardship committee to come to the meeting on Thursday evening. Ya'll come!"

Different events in the congregation, depending upon their intent and appeal, exert differing levels of attraction. A small attendance does not necessarily mean an unsuccessful gathering. All the members of the Women's Aid Executive committee, for example, knew who they were. A "ya'll come" announcement under such circumstances is quite sufficient. The recruitment of an effective stewardship committee, or any major committee, however, does not happen by chance. A "ya'll come" announcement might be a good way to inform the congregation. But when a specific concern is to be discussed or a specific task performed, the church should recruit leaders with expertise in related areas.

Barb went to her pastor early in the spring to volunteer to lead Bible school.

The pastor was aghast. "You're an answer to a prayer!" he said. Barb had made his day. The next few months would be much easier with this new "assistant" helping with the program. The previous year, the Vacation Bible School director had nearly burned out as a result of the arduous task, but Barb would make it work.

The previous director had contacted more than a hundred people to get just a handful to agree to help. Barb completed her staff well over a month before the program was to begin. Not one person she contacted declined. Was it her personality? Perhaps, in part. Was it the way she asked? Perhaps, in part. Was it who she asked? Probably not. Many of the same people had been contacted the year before. Was it her approach? Probably, to a large degree. Barb was inviting people to be a part of something she really believed in. It was not just a task to be accomplished. It was a ministry to be done. She was committed—and she had done her homework and planning.

2. Creative Visioning and Planning. The second golden thread of effective leadership is commitment to visioning and planning. Visioning, coupled with solid planning, is the "stuff" that enables mission and ministry to happen. These two elements—visioning and planning—are foundational. They get results because they ask the right questions.

What are the goals? Five solid goals for a good stewardship program might include:
- Raise in members the level of consciousness about stewardship as it relates to our whole life.
- Disconnect the stewardship appeal from the budget process of the congregation by allowing the budget to flow from the appeal.
- Build an awareness that our stewardship involves giving an amount in proportion to our income.
- Significantly raise the level of giving by members of the congregation by emphasizing proportionate giving and tithing.
- Measure the increase accurately so that a realistic budget can be developed.

What is the task?
- What specific events make up the calendar leading up to commitment time?
- How many separate functions are needed to make this program a success?
- Are enough people involved so that no one needs to fulfill more than one or two simple tasks?

What is the proper sequence of the task in order to accomplish the goal?
- Effective church leaders know that any goal needs to be reduced to its simplest level.
- What steps are necessary to reach the goal?
- Is recruitment really the first thing to be done, or would it be better to approach people with a more specific request, following further planning?
- Strategizing creates a step-by-step approach to complete the goal and includes intermediate deadlines.

3. Creative Communication. "Why does the pastor stand up there every Sunday morning during the announcements and tell us everything that's in the bulletin?" whispered Lydia. "Let's get on with the service."

Her sister, with that "shush" look, wrote on her bulletin, "It's because nobody ever reads the bulletin."

"Well, there has to be a better way to make us aware of what is going on than standing up there and reading it to us. How's that going to encourage people to read it? Everyone knows we don't have to read it. He's going to read it to us!"

Lydia is right, of course. Repeating everything a church bulletin contains does not encourage people to read it. Yet the pastor had learned that the congregation was not convinced that something was important unless he drew special attention to it. Messages regarding stewardship, if we really intend to communicate them, require variety and pizzazz. We do not transmit information unless we first get attention.

Action Possibilities:
- Stewardship is not rated "M"—for mature audiences only. When making a stewardship announcement, invite members of the youth group, the committee, or other involved persons to help give it a flare. Brief skits can be helpful ways to communicate. Acting out an important announcement, even if it also is in the bulletin, can call special attention to it more effectively than if the pastor merely reiterates the printed material.
- Pay close attention to the way announcements of importance are placed in the bulletin. Many congregations, concerned about space and the need to avoid too many pages, cram the bulletin so full that it is nearly unreadable. If you are planning a stewardship dinner, it may deserve its own insert. Computer graphics, clip art, and different typefaces (fonts) also help to focus attention on important events.

4. *Creative Coordination.* An old story tells about an argument among the instruments of an orchestra. The bassoon boasted that its mellow, deep-throated voice gave body to the music. The violin chipped in that without it, the melody would fizzle. The kettledrum thundered that without it, the power of the *1812 Overture* would come across like a cap pistol. The flute, looking sideways at the violin, commented that it could provide a softness to the music that the violins could never give.

The oboe squawked derisively and commented, "Without me, you'd all be out of tune. It's my piercing tuning note that gets the orchestra started right." The argument raged on, with each instrument getting in its two-cents worth.

After a time the conductor scowled, "How can any of you be more essential than essential? Each of you plays a key role at one time or another, but unless you all work together, there can be no music."

The orchestra was dumbfounded. "No music! What would the world be like without music!" cried the trumpet with a fanfare. "That's our whole purpose in being!"

There is no "most important ministry" in the church. Unless stewardship is coordinated with all the other work of the congregation, it will come across like an oboe with a broken reed. Contacting other committees and task groups with your plans for the stewardship program is not merely a courtesy; it is a necessity. The more other church leaders know about what is going on in the stewardship corner, the more effective the stewardship program will be. The more the stewardship committee is aware of the contributions of the other departments, the more it will help to strengthen the whole program of the church.

Learn from the Geese

Fact: As a goose flaps its wings, it creates an uplift for the bird following. By flying in a "V" formation, the whole flock adds 71 percent more flying range than if each bird flew alone.

Lesson: Christian people share a common direction and sense of community. Churches can get where they are going more quickly and easily if they travel upon the thrust of one another.

Action Possibility: Stewardship is foundational to the ministries accomplished by all task groups in the congregation. Each committee has a captivating stewardship story to tell. Stewardship committee members profit from inviting the chairperson of each committee to attend one meeting each year. The agenda for the entire meeting might involve a listening time for the stewardship-committee members. This would enable everyone to gain an overview of the ministries of each committee. Everyone could reflect about how the work of each committee contributes to other ministry areas.

Fact: Whenever a goose falls out of formation, it suddenly feels the drag and resistance of trying to fly alone. It quickly gets back into formation to take advantage of the uplifting power of the birds immediately in front.

Lesson: If we have as much sense as these birds, we will join in formations with those who are headed where we want to go.

Action Possibility: The work of the governing board enhances the coordination of information. It is also helpful for stewardship committee members to hear a monthly report from the board representative about any new directions from other committees. This will keep members from "bucking the head winds."

Fact: When the lead goose is tired, it rotates back into the formation and another goose flies at the point position.

Lesson: It pays to take turns with the vital tasks and in sharing leadership. With people as with geese, interdependence with one another makes ministry both more exciting and more fruitful.

Action Possibility: During the stewardship appeal, it is a good rule of thumb that *no one* take on more than one or two simple tasks.

Fact: The geese in formation honk from behind to encourage those up front to keep up their speed.

Lesson: We need to make sure that our "honking from behind" is encouraging rather than critical.

Action Possibility: When reporting the results of a stewardship appeal to members of the congregation, it is imperative that members of the congregation (1) be thanked; (2) be praised for new ministry that will be accomplished; and (3) be informed of visions that the congregation still hopes to accomplish.

Fact: When a goose is sick, wounded, or shot down, two geese drop out of formation and follow it down to help and provide protection. They stay with this fellow member of the flock until it either is able to fly again or dies. Then they launch out on their own, join another formation, or try to catch up with their own flock.

Lesson: If we have as much common sense as these birds, we too will stand by one another.

Action Possibility: Team work is effective because it accomplishes more, while seeming like less work. When you are tempted to do a Lone Ranger stewardship emphasis, evaluate that inclination carefully. Flying in formation is a bit less glamorous, but you are far more likely to arrive at your destination and far less likely to end up as a cooked goose.

IX

WILL I HAVE TO MAKE VISITS?

Sara Greene sat on the couch in her living room, her eyes wide as those of a newborn fawn. Her cold clammy hands were gripped tightly between her knees. What she had just heard had been the one thing she had never expected to hear. It wasn't bad news . . . at least, she didn't think so. Her husband, Derek, sat beside her in a much more relaxed state, amused at the intensity of her reaction. Across from them, in a too-large overstuffed chair, sat their pastor. He did not have to be psychic to realize that his request had caught Sara by surprise.

"Sara," he said, "I have to tell you that I consider the stewardship committee as important to the ministry of our congregation as the church's governing board."

Sara looked up at him, still feeling an odd sensation in her stomach. If she had not known better, she would have assumed it was caused by something she had eaten.

The pastor went on, "You seem a little surprised, Sara."

"*Aghast* would be a better term, Pastor," she said, her voice seeming to quiver a bit. "It's just one of those things I've never even considered. I mean, yes, I deal with money every day in my work. And if you'd said finance commit-

tee, I'd have been more prepared. But stewardship committee?"

"As I said," continued the pastor, "I think it's perhaps the
most important committee in the church."

"I know you mean that, but before you came to our
church, there wasn't even a stewardship committee. I've
been in other churches that had them, but the thought of
serving on one just gives me the chills."

"Why do you think that might be?" he asked, already
knowing the answer, but wanting to give her a chance to put
her feelings into words.

"Well, I suppose I've always thought of the stewardship
committee as a group of very extroverted people who go out
and knock on doors and ask people for more money. Would
I have to *make visits?*"

The pastor smiled. "I won't suggest that the committee
will never decide to make visits. I can tell you that calls
aren't normally a part of our regular stewardship appeals. If
we ever do a capital-fund drive, then there likely will be
visits. My guess is that the first time we have an Every Member Visitation, it would be to share the mission story of the
church.

"If we were to make personal contacts, it would be up to
every individual to decide whether to participate in the calling. Being a member of the committee would not obligate
you to make calls. On the other hand, we will provide special training for those who do, and most people say they
really enjoy the visits."

"Would I have to ask people for money?" queried Sara.

"Most of the time, our asking is not on a one-to-one
basis. That's usually only a part of the EMV. We might ask
members to share articles for the newsletter, or possibly
make a stewardship talk, but it would be entirely up to
them."

"I'm a bit of an introvert, pastor. Getting up in front of
people puts my nerves into hyperspace."

"That's okay. There are many things you can do on the

committee without being in the public eye. We've given careful thought to the people we are inviting. We want the best. With your background and your family's commitment to Christ, we thought you would be good."

Sara looked at her husband. "Did you know about this?"

"Well, when your name came up, I told them you would have to decide for yourself. I thought the pastor should ask you because he knows more about what's involved."

"You don't have to decide tonight, Sara. Take a few days to think and pray about it, if you wish."

"I guess that's not really necessary. But be forewarned. If I decide I can't hack it, I'll ask out."

"I take it that's a yes?"

"Well, okay. I mean yes, but you'd better be praying very hard," smiled Sara.

"I promise! Thank you, Sara, and thank you, Derek, for your support for her."

Sara's story is not unusual. Many congregations have some difficulty recruiting members for the stewardship committee. Quite often, invitations to serve on a stewardship committee result in a "What? Who, me?" response. An almost universal fear people have about serving is that they will have to "ask" someone for money.

Churches with high levels of giving realize that lay people usually do not like to visit other lay people *solely* to ask for money. These churches also know that some people fear public speaking—especially to talk about stewardship.

Stewardship committees do more than just raise money. Their overall ministry goal is to enhance the level of vision for ministry. The ministry of stewardship is accomplished in four basic ways. While the annual stewardship appeal contains all four elements, that once-a-year task is only a small part of an effective committee's work.

Four Building Blocks for Stewardship Development

1. Leadership. Leaders lead best by example. What people do is far more powerful than what they say. The first requirement for members of a stewardship committee is, therefore, that they be personally committed to Jesus Christ. This will result in commitment to the ministry to which our Lord calls us through the church. Growth for committee members should always be part of the agenda, but commitment should be a prerequisite for joining the team.

Stewardship is both caught and taught. A second requisite for an effective stewardship leader, therefore, is that one be a faithful steward. People who are committed to stewardship are committed to giving. This involves a willingness to follow the biblical principles of percentage giving and tithing. It also includes a willingness to stand up and be counted. Members of stewardship committees should be people who make estimates of their giving.

Leadership in stewardship ministry rests primarily with the pastor and the members of the stewardship committee. But other leaders play an essential role too. A congregation's governing body holds the final authority in most congregations. Members of this group also should be challenged to practice sacrificial stewardship and make their commitments up front. If the elected leaders of a church do not lead, how can they expect the followers to follow?

2. Education. Stewardship education consists of teaching people the biblical principles of stewardship. This means communicating an understanding that all we have is a gift from God. Christians are called to manage these gifts. Everything we have, from the water we drink to the children God has given us, is the Lord's. We are called to use, care for, and share those gifts according to God's purposes. Our stewardship is a joyful and grateful response to all that God has done in our lives. Stewardship education is accomplished through sermons, Bible studies, personal witness, Christian education programs, Sunday school, and confirmation classes. The use of audiovisual presentations also enhances stewardship education.

The stewardship committee in one congregation had agreed to work with the parish education committee to offer a series of Sunday school classes during the time of the annual appeal. All adult classes were asked to be a part of this four-week series. The church sent a letter to all adults in the congregation, notifying them of the change. (They also hoped that some who did not come regularly to Sunday school would attend this four-week series.)

A few days later, the pastor received a sharp note from one woman in the congregation. She wrote, "I don't think we need to study about stewardship. We already know everything there is to know about it—at least I do."

Church members who do not need to study stewardship are about as plentiful as those who have memorized the entire Bible. Fortunately, more people are coming to see the advantages of looking carefully at what the Bible says about stewardship. Pastors report that members are even asking for such classes. In congregations where tithing has not been emphasized for many years, members are delighted when a pastor or committee picks up the banner.

3. Interpretation. Theoretically, all Christians should need only an acquaintance with the *why* we give.

A woman once said, "It's a shame that Christian people don't give just because they love the Lord. That should be sufficient to initiate an overflow of sharing—*solely* as a response to God's love. Why all the need for campaigns and appeals?" While one can appreciate her enthusiasm, not all Christians have attained that level of maturity.

American Christians always seem to want to know where their money is going. And that is good, to a point. Stewardship interpretation helps people know and understand the causes, ministries, and programs to which they give.

Churches owe accountability to their people for the way they use the Lord's gifts. People want to know also because they are interested in the mission and ministry of their church.

Offerings given to God in the Old Testament most often were not for special needs and causes. A portion of those offerings were even burned. People sometimes made sacrifices just because they knew that everyone needed to give. Just as in Old Testament times, Christian people today need to give. But they will also need interpretation regarding where the giving goes—if leaders expect that giving level to remain high.

4. *Opportunities to Give.* The stewardship committee is responsible for giving each member ample opportunity to make financial faith responses. Stewardship committees should, therefore, never apologize for asking. Each Christian makes the decision about the opportunities to which he or she can or cannot contribute. It is *not* the responsibility of the committee or of the pastor to protect the pocketbook of any member. People are perfectly capable of protecting their own. Generally speaking, if someone complains, "We're constantly asking for money—it's just one appeal after another," well and good! The committee is doing its job.

Special Offerings

Special offerings should be viewed by congregations and committees as special opportunities to give. They are occasions for accomplishing ministry in new and different ways. No congregation can foresee every situation or crisis that can arise during the year. No one can know about disasters around the world that may call for a response from Christian people. Committees should be aware that there are at least five positive reasons for special offerings.

1. Special offerings are biblical. The apostle Paul wrote, "Now concerning the contribution for the saints: as I directed the churches of Galatia, so you also are to do. . . . And when I arrive, I will send those whom you accredit by letter to carry your gift to Jerusalem" (I Cor. 16:1, 3 RSV). In Romans 15:26, he continues, "For Macedonia and Achaia have been pleased to make some contribution for the poor among the saints at Jerusalem" (RSV). Paul did not fear special offerings. Neither should we.

2. The givers with the highest potential will not be challenged by regular budgetary giving. One out of every 426 Americans is a millionaire. Some people have such large incomes that they can spend one-third, give one-third, and save one-third. For every forty giving units in a church, there is one unit capable of making a one-time gift equal to the church's budget. If no one ever asks them, they are not likely to think of giving it to the church. Instead, they will think of giving it to a university, a hospital, or some other worthy cause. Why? Because those institutions will think to ask. Such people will, however, contribute to special offerings over and above their regular budgetary gifts.

3. Special offerings attract money that otherwise would not have been given. This is especially true of capital-improvements campaigns. Two factors need to be in place: (a) There should be a reasonably good consensus among members that "we need" this improvement; (b) An effective program must be used to gather the gifts and pledges. When these two conditions are met, the total amount of immediate gifts and three-year pledges will equal or exceed two and one-half times the amount normally received in one year for the church's annual budget. Very little of this additional money would be given without a special appeal.

4. Special offerings attract designated mission money that would not have been given through a unified budget.

For example, 20 percent of the Christian Church (Disciples of Christ) annual denominational giving comes from special-day offerings. Such special days in all denominations are educational because people *read* the material—often one of the few times they ever *read* something about what their denomination is doing.

5. Regular giving normally comes from current income. Special offerings, such as a major-gifts portion of an appeal, attract money primarily from members' accumulated assets. For the "average" family in most congregations, only 15 percent of its net worth is current income; 85 percent of its net worth is accumulated resources.

Some people object to special offerings because they fear that the congregation may experience a falling off of regular giving during a special appeal. Three facts should be kept in mind: (a) When receiving a special offering, the advance publicity needs to strongly urge the people to remember that the offering is "over and above" their regular giving; (b) Even when regular giving falls a bit, the actual total receipts are usually higher, because the appeal will enhance the total giving; (c) If the special appeal is of long duration, such as a three-year capital-fund drive, leaders can encourage the members to "roll over" that special giving into another ministry area at the end of the three years.

One More Opportunity to Give— Stewardship After Life

Christian people are Christians for life . . . and beyond. When we commit ourselves to Jesus Christ, we do so knowing that this is an eternal commitment. Christian stewardship is no different. We will want to give as God blesses us, for as long as God blesses us. Many Christian people, therefore, think about how they can continue their giving even after their life is over in this world.

One way to be a steward after life is to remember the church, denomination, Christian college or university, or charitable institution in your will. This means that stewardship committees should keep in mind that part of their responsibility in providing opportunities to give is to invite people to give through effective planning of their estate.

Action Possibilities:
- Offer every member the information needed to write a will or to revise an old will. Have information available on how to make gifts with life insurance, life-income agreements, and payable-on-death accounts.
- Urge every member to ask, "Should I remember my church in my will? Should I include a ministry of my denomination or the denomination itself? Should I remember an institution of the church such as a social-service agency, camping ministries, church colleges and universities, or seminaries?"
- Restructure your efforts to include estate planning as an integral part of your church's ongoing stewardship program, rather than making it a perhaps once-in-a-decade special effort.
- Consider holding a Life After Life workshop in your congregation. Invite all members to attend this wills-awareness event. Remind people that if they are married or of legal age, they should have an estate plan in place. Invite an estate planner from a Christian college or institution and an attorney knowledgeable of charitable bequests to help conduct the seminar.

This can benefit both the congregation and the donor, for people like to remember their church in their will. In fact, it often provides an incentive for people who otherwise are reluctant to write a will.

A word of caution: It is important for a congregation to have in place some kind of endowment/trust document that outlines how moneys received in a bequest will be used. Congregations that receive a large bequest without such a plan often tell war stories of the congregation's income falling off after a large gift. If an endowment/trust fund is in place, such a gift can be a blessing. If it is not, a bequest sometimes can wreak havoc in the congregation's stewardship ministry. (See Appendix E for further informa tion on preparing a congregational endowment/trust fund.)

"You can't teach an old dog like me new tricks," said Charlie. "I'm just not sure about this stewardship-committee thing. I've served on almost every other committee in the church, but this is one I've avoided like the plague. It's not that I don't believe in stewardship. You know I do! It's just that, to me, it seems so ominous to be on that committee."

Sara sat smiling, remembering last year, when she had sat in her living room in a state of near panic.

"Okay, what's the joke?" asked Charlie.

"I was just thinking back," Sara replied. "Just one year ago, the pastor asked the same question of me. I don't think anything he could have asked would have surprised me more. In fact, I only agreed because I couldn't think of any legitimate reason to say no."

"I've got one," said Charlie.

"Oh? What is it?" asked Sara, knowing she'd probably heard it before.

"I don't know anything about being on a stewardship committee. I'd be a handicap to the rest of the group. If I can't make a contribution to a committee, what's the point in taking up a chair?"

"None of us are experts. In fact, we're all learning at every meeting. At the beginning of every meeting, for the first half-hour after devotions, we do a stewardship study together. Sometimes we take a good stewardship book and discuss it together. We read it at home, and come prepared to discuss. The pastor or a committee member leads the discussion, and we have a grand ol' time. There's just one good reason why we want you on this committee, Charlie."

"What's that?" asked Charlie in a still small voice.

"You're a good steward. You practice biblical steward-ship. You tithe, and your whole life-style reflects that you are a mature Christian. That's why we want you. Technical expertise can come later. The most important things you can bring to the committee are commitment to Jesus Christ and the desire to grow. You see, Charlie, we old dogs can learn a lot of new tricks on this committee."

"Well, Sara, when they picked you to ask me, they picked the right person. I guess you've got a new committee member!"

ASK THE VITAL QUESTION

"Clarence, all this church ever does is ask for money!" exclaimed an inactive member. "I'd come a lot more if I thought they were after more than just what's in my pocketbook."

"You know, John, I used to think that too. In fact, for years I used it as an excuse to stay away from church. Then sitting in my living room one night, I said that very thing to a visitor from church. And what he said got me to thinking."

"I'm not sure I want to ask what he said," replied Ernie.

"Gotcha! The mere fact that you're not sure you want to know suggests to me that maybe you're not so sure of that comment."

"Guess you've got a point there," said Ernie. Folding his arms across his chest with a sheepish grin, he went on, "Okay, reach me!"

"Well, don't forget that this is unrehearsed. I didn't expect you to make that comment. I'm not a professional, you know."

"That's okay, but am I wrong? The church does ask its members to give. The pastor does preach about money quite a bit."

"So did Jesus, Ernie. In fact, our Lord talked about money more than any single subject except the kingdom of God itself. Actually, our pastor doesn't preach more than about half a dozen sermons a year that even deal with money. Come to think of it, I can hardly remember when he ever talked about money when the lessons didn't bring it up. Our pastor usually talks about the missions that our money is given for."

"What's the difference?"

"Actually, it's not the church that is always asking for money—it's the world. When was the last time you went to a store and the clerk didn't ask you for money? It was assumed. Ernie, you run a store. You wouldn't think of *not* expecting a customer to pay for your services."

"Well, yes, but a customer gets something in return."

"Isn't helping other people something in return? I get something in return every Sunday when I know that the money I place in the offering plate is going to help somebody. I know I'm helping provide for some special ministry and enabling our church to carry out the ministry God wants us to do.

"Another thing my visitor said," Clarence continued, "was that I get a whole stack of bills each month, each from someone expecting money. Are any of them from the church? We don't even send out bills for pledges that are past due.

"And who withholds a percentage of your earnings every paycheck? It's not your heavenly Father. It's your uncle!

"There's no free lunch anywhere—except at church. There's no admission charge. Seats in church are free. If you get sick, the pastor will call on you. If your son or daughter gets married, the church will be there for them. Our church newsletter goes out every month. But no one ever gets a subscription notice.

"When your wife died a couple of years ago, you paid the funeral home. But the church didn't expect anything, except to be there for you when you needed it. In fact, the church will always be there for you—clean, heated, and glad to be of service. And no one but a select few will ever even know

124

if you contributed or not. Just think! Compared to the gov-
ernment and bill collectors, the church very seldom asks for
money. Yet, of all the things your money could be used for,
very few are as important as what the church provides."

"Okay, Clarence, I guess you've got me feeling a little
ashamed. In fact, maybe the church should ask for money a
little more."

"Well, we do, but just not every Sunday. Once each year
we have an opportunity to make our estimate of giving for
the coming twelve months. Each of us is asked to look at
what God has done for us, and how we've been blessed, and
give accordingly. And the pastor and church leaders are not
bashful about bringing to our attention other special opportunities for giving. That's as it should be.

"My point is this: Compared to the rest of the world, we
ask very little. But people give a lot—not because we ask,
but because they want to. God wants our heart first. Unless
our giving comes from the heart, we haven't learned how to
be good stewards. That's what stewardship is all about—
asking for the heart. Surely that is positive. Surely churches
should do more of that, not less!"

Churches with high levels of giving realize that most people *do not* increase their giving unless someone asks them to
do so on an annual basis. Conversely, churches with high
giving levels understand that people like to give and usually
will respond favorably when asked. Contrary to the popular
myth, most members are *not* offended when money is
requested.

The good news is that most people will not *decrease* their
giving, even if they are *not* asked annually. They tend to
keep giving at the same levels. The bad news is that they will
not grow in their giving unless they are asked. The worse
news is that there will not be sufficient money to accomplish
the ministries that God calls churches to do unless people
grow in their giving. This means that "annual asking" is
absolutely essential to effective stewardship leadership and
to the effectiveness of congregational ministries.

The Invisible Demons

Two invisible demons affect the income of every individual and every congregation. They lurk in the halls and behind the walls of every home and every church in the land. Like a poltergeist, they play tricks on our logic—attempting to shrivel and shrink our money. They show no partiality, affecting Christians and unbelievers alike. Most of all, they modify the amount of money we give to our Lord by deceiving us into thinking that we give more than we actually do.

The first of these invisible demons is *inflation*. Everyone knows about this demon, yet so often it does not come into our thinking when it is time to consider increasing our giving. Inflation does some amazing things to our money. To use a round figure, examine $100,000 of church income in different years, to find out what it needed to be in 1990, just to continue the same ministry. That amount—$100,000—in 1980 shrank so much that by 1990, roughly $161,174 was needed to provide the same ministry. Going back farther enables us to see the more drastic effects of inflation. A church with a $100,000 income in 1975 would need roughly $246,960 to provide the same ministry in 1990. Going back another ten years to 1965, $100,000 would mean that a church needed to receive $421,209 in 1990.

In the past twenty-five years, spending power has dropped so drastically that we need more than four times as much income to continue the same ministry. Yet, many congregations tend to plod along, paralyzed by the myth that we "just can't ask our people for more money." The demon of inflation mandates that congregations *must* grow in giving—and at a rate that exceeds inflation—in order to enable any new ministries to begin.

The second invisible demon is *interest* on loans. Loans are a reality and, for many congregations, a necessary evil. At times, mission requires that we borrow money to accomplish what God calls us to do. Lord of Life Church is a mission congregation. It had its beginning in the somewhat inadequate auditorium of a school. In spite of less-than-ideal conditions, the congregation continued to grow. Financial growth, however, outstripped its growth in members. The second year of its existence netted a 28.5 percent stewardship increase over the first year. The next year, giving jumped by an additional 47 percent. Year four netted another 26 percent increase in dollars, in spite of a slower growth in membership.

Experts assured the church that if growth in new members was to approach the growth in income, a more adequate worship facility was needed. The growth patterns experienced by new congregations of other denominations in the neighborhood seemed to verify that observation. Eight months after receiving the third consecutive increase, the church conducted a capital-fund drive and received a handsome three-year commitment from the members. That commitment, however, was not adequate to complete the first worship unit, so borrowing money became a necessity for mission.

While interest is not entirely invisible, it tends to be hidden from everyday scrutiny, since it usually is tied in with principal and payments. Below is a chart that includes various amounts borrowed for periods of fifteen, twenty, and thirty years.[20]

	Principal plus Interest @ 10%	Total Interest Paid	Average Interest per Year
	$75,000 Mortgage		
15 Years	$145,071.00	$70,071.00	$4,671.40
20 Years	173,704.80	98,704.80	4,935.24
30 Years	236,944.80	161,944.80	5,398.16
	$250,000 Mortgage		
15 Years	$483,571.80	$233,571.80	$15,571.45

	Principal plus Interest @ 10%	Total Interest Paid	Average Interest per Year
20 Years	579,012.00	329,012.00	16,450.60
30 Years	789,814.80	539,814.80	17,993.83
	$500,000 Mortgage		
15 Years	$967,145.40	$467,145.40	$31,143.03
20 Years	1,158,026.40	658,026.40	32,901.32
30 Years	1,579,629.60	1,079,629.60	35,987.65

Average interest per year is shown on the chart above for the sake of comparison. Most actual interest on loans, however, is paid early in the loan period. Using the above chart with a $75,000 fifteen-year mortgage, the monthly payment would be $805.95. Of that payment, $625 would be interest, with the remaining $180.95 attacking the principal. Near the end of the loan, of course, the figures would almost reverse.

Both inflation and interest are part of the cost of doing ministry. Congregations, however, need to use every possible opportunity to minimize the negative impact of these two money eaters.

Action Possibilities:
- Seek to minimize the impact of inflation by keeping people aware of the added cost of doing the same ministry from year to year. A newsletter article, a stewardship talk early in the year, and the pastor's attention to the concern will help congregations realize that congregational income must go up if we continue the ministry we carried out the previous year. Cost of denominational ministries is also affected. Benevolence, too, must continue to rise.
- Before borrowing any money, conduct a thorough capital-funds appeal. If the amount needed is large, profes-

sional stewardship directors are often available to help
with the appeal. There is usually a cost for such services, but the results will easily justify it. Appeals of
this type often include a three-year commitment. Since
the money often is not adequate to cover the entire cost
of the building, and since only a small portion is available "up front," borrowing still usually will be a necessity.

• When borrowing money, look to other avenues before
using commercial loans. Nearly every congregation has
at least one member who could write a check for the
entire church budget. Try first to borrow from members
at low and simple interest. This can help to offset the
amount needed before the money is given.

• The mission of the church is not to pay interest to
financial institutions. One extra payment per year on
a 30-year mortgage can reduce the total length of payments to approximately 22 years. Ask four neighboring congregations of your denomination to join you in
helping a local mission congregation build its first
worship facility. Each church would agree to pay the
equivalent of one payment per year directly to the
principal of the mission congregation's loan. This
would reduce its mortgage from 30 years to approximately 11 years. On a $500,000 mortgage at 10 percent
interest, this method pays an additional $240,000
directly to the principal. Those payments save more
than $750,000 in interest payments over the life of the
mortgage—money that can be put into mission. Following the retirement of the loan, the mission congregation could repay the other congregations. Better
still, the new congregation could continue to make
payments into a mission investment fund of its denomination, so that other congregations might receive a similar type of help. Thus these payments that would have
been lost to interest can accomplish mission by helping
others.[21]

Dispel the Myth

One of the most deadly *myths* of stewardship is, "Pastor, we don't dare keep asking our people for more money!" This myth may come up in a variety of ways for a variety of reasons. Since the cost of everything else is rising, people may honestly *mis*-believe that the church should counter by not asking members to sacrifice further. Because they are giving at a sacrificial level, other members *mis*-believe that all in the congregation are doing their best as well. Another major *mis*-belief is that "the church doesn't really need the money. If we give more, they'll just spend it." In addition, of course, honesty would force us to classify some members as "tight." Not every Christian is at the same level of maturity in the walk of faith.

Arguing these topics with ardent *mis*-believers is usually counterproductive. However, asking questions when people make such comments is appropriate and often helpful.

"I think we're all in favor of making our building more accessible to our older people," commented Brian, "but we just have to remember that we can't continue to keep asking our people for more money. Our members are getting older, and some are on fixed-incomes. Candy, you're a member of the stewardship committee. What do you think?"

"Well, Brian, you've made a couple of very good points," responded Candy, and watched Brian beam with satisfaction. "There are a couple of concerns we need to address. First, I think we'll all agree that you're right that almost no one in our congregation would vote against making our building fully accessible to those with handicapsif the money were available. Second, our members are getting older. In the next ten years, 50 percent of our present membership will be over the age of sixty.

"However, in an income survey we did last spring, we found that very few members of our church are on what can legitimately be called a fixed-income. In fact, in our community, retirement incomes seldom decrease over pre-retirement incomes. Members may not continue after retirement to get as much of an increase in their income during each year as they did before, but retirement doesn't necessarily mean *lower* income."

"But Candy, my point was that we can't keep asking people for more money. Don't you agree with that?"

"Not completely, Brian. As a member of the stewardship committee, I see my role as one of informing members of opportunities for ministry. We're the voice and ears of our church. Our job is to make our members aware of what we think God is calling us to do. Neither the stewardship committee nor the governing board should be a guardian of our members' pocketbooks. Members are perfectly capable of guarding their own. People will rarely give so sacrificially that they give beyond their capability. On the other hand, the income survey revealed that the members of our church are giving just 3.4 percent of their annual income."

"Wow, that's a far cry from a tithe," gulped Brian. "Maybe I was mistaken. Maybe we should be asking our members to grow." (See Appendix B for instructions on how to survey your congregation's potential.)

Action Possibilities:
- Prepare stewardship-committee members for dealing with these myths by taking some of the committee's study time at the beginning of meetings to discuss them. Make a list of the reasons these myths are not true. Ask committee members to report on these discussions with the church's governing body or through newsletter articles.
- Counter the myths about stewardship in ways and at times when it is nonthreatening to do so. It is a grievous error to argue about a myth when a member passionately and piously announces it as a "fact of life." Approaching the subject when it will threaten no one may gain an audience from the most ardent mis-

believer. Newsletter articles, as well as fun and educational skits by youth members, are ways to counter myths and edify members.

Ask the Question Right

Asking the right question is important, but asking the question right is crucial.

Seven-year-old Robbie came scampering into the house after school with his arms so loaded that he could hardly see where he was going.

"Hi Mom, I'm home," he announced as he proudly dumped his load on the kitchen table. "Look what I've got!"

"Wow! What's all that?" asked his mother.

"Our school has three kinds of things we can sell to make money for our new playground. Besides that, if we sell the most, we get some other prizes too. Look at this picture of the skateboard I'm going to earn. We could choose which of these things we wanted to sell, but I decided I'd sell all three, and that would give me more points toward the skateboard."

"Oh, and how do you expect to sell all this stuff?" asked Mom.

"I got it all figured out," Robbie explained. "Since Dad's a salesman, I figured I'd just ask him to take it to his office and get the other salespeople to buy it."

"Interesting plan," replied Mom, "but it's up to you to ask your dad."

Just then Robbie heard his dad's car turning in the driveway. He rushed out to meet him with that "I want something" look on his face.

After running through his entire spiel, he asked, "Would you take this with you to work and ask the others at your office to buy some?"

"Not a chance. Tell you what I will do, though. I'll take you to work, and you can ask them yourself. This Saturday morning there's a meeting, and we'll all be there a little early, so while I'm getting some stuff ready for the meeting, you can go around and make your sales. Fair enough?"

The time between that night and Saturday morning seemed like an eternity to Robbie, but on the big day, he was up and ready an hour before his parents. On the way to work, his dad coached him a bit about what to say when he went up to each staff member.

When they arrived, Rob walked bravely up to each salesperson and said, "Hi, I'm Robbie and I'm selling these three items so my school can get some new playground equipment, and so I can win this gorgeous skateboard. How much would you like to order?" He sold $97.00 worth, and all but one person ordered something.

Churches are not in the sales business, but they can learn some lessons from young Robert. First, he kept a positive approach. Second, he assumed that when the people had all the information, they would want to buy. Third, he learned from his father that a good salesperson does not ask a "Yes or No" question. People want to be a part of the ministry done by their church.

The question should never be, "Will you increase your giving next year?" or worse, "Shall we put you down for the same amount as last year?" Rather, it should be, "How much will you grow in your giving for the next twelve months?"

Christian people like to give. When they are well-informed about the congregation's ministries and are asked to grow, the vast majority will respond favorably.

APPENDIX A

CHECKLIST FOR VITAL STEWARDSHIP

_____ 1. Are we basing our appeal on a sound, positive biblical foundation, rather than on a budget-building or institutional foundation?

_____ 2. Do we have a holistic understanding of stewardship in our congregation?

    _____ • Does our congregation have a year-round plan for stewardship education?

    _____ • Do we conduct a stewardship campaign *every* year?

    _____ • Are we sensitive to people's desire to give beyond their lifetime by providing an effective endowment-trust vehicle, to enable bequests without harming our ongoing stewardship ministry?

_____ 3. Does our pastor provide effective leadership for our stewardship ministry?

    _____ • by providing both theological and methodological leadership?

    _____ • by stressing the biblical teachings of tithing and percentage giving?

    _____ • by setting a strong example of stewardship in her/his personal life?

_____ 4. Realizing that in congregations where members estimate their giving, and those who do estimate give about 30 percent more than those who do not, do we have an effective plan by which we ask our members to estimate their giving?

_____ 5. Have we been careful to utilize fully existing step-by-step how-to-do-it programs, rather than asking the stewardship committee to design our annual campaign?

If the stewardship committee has decided to design our own campaign, have we begun the planning at least six months before execution begins?

If the stewardship committee has decided to design our own campaign, have we taken the precaution of writing it out step by step?

_____ 6. Do we concentrate on the _need of the giver to give_, rather than on the _need of our congregation to receive_, especially during our annual stewardship campaign?

_____ 7. Have we heeded the admonition to change our campaign approach every two or three years?

Have we taken care not to delete _anything_ from the printed stewardship programs we use?

_____ 8. Have we involved a sufficient number of lay leaders in executing the annual stewardship plan, so that no person will undertake more than one or two obligations during the appeal?

_____ 9. How have we taken into consideration people's built-in reluctance to visiting other people _solely_ for the purpose of asking for money?

If we conduct an Every-Home Visit, are we taking care that the visitors share the vision for mission of the church, rather than merely requesting money for the budget?

_____ 10. Knowing that most members will not grow in their giving unless asked to do so annually, how effectively have we presented the invitation to grow in their personal stewardship of financial blessings?

APPENDIX B

ANALYZING YOUR CONGREGATION'S POTENTIAL

The apostle Paul had a great suggestion! He encouraged the congregation in Corinth to give *in proportion to what they had earned.* That is an important New Testament concept:

PERCENTAGE GIVING!

	Example	Your Congregation
1. In this congregation, the number of households is:	125	————
2. The median (EBI)* household income is:	$26,122	————
3. The total income of congregational members is: (1 x 2 = ___)	$3,266,625	————
4. Last year, the total giving was:	$75,133	————
5. This means that the average giving per household was:		
Dollars: (Divide line 4 by line 1)	$601	————
Percent: (Divide line 4 by line 3)	2.3%	————

	Example	Your Congregation
6. If each household increased its giving by 1% of the household income next year, the congregation would receive: (Add 1% to line 6 and multiply by line 3)	$99,176	————
7. Dollar and percentage increase next year: (Dollar: Subtract line 4 from line 6;	$24,043	————
Percentage: Subtract line 7 from line 4 and divide by line 4)	32%	————

Think of the potential for mission if even a large portion of your members grow each year in their giving to the church by one percent of their income! What would happen if even 30 percent or 50 percent began to tithe their incomes? (And these calculations are based on income after taxes. What if members followed the biblical principle of God first and gave from their gross income?)

*EBI is Effective Buying Income (i.e., income minus taxes—federal, state, and local). NOTE: Median EBI per household means that there are as many households above the stated income figure as below it. These figures can be obtained from your local library, the Chamber of Commerce, and from *Sales and Marketing Management* magazine.

APPENDIX C

PREPARING A VISION FOR MINISTRY

NOTE: A Vision for Ministry is one way to effectively communicate the mission of your congregation. The following is just one approach to preparing a brochure for presenting your congregation's Vision for Ministry. Use your imagination and adapt it in any way that seems to fit your needs. When calculating financial figures, if you should use them, include staff salaries under each category, in proportion to the time spent by staff in each ministry area.

PAGE 1 — LETTER FROM PASTOR(S)

PAGE 2 — A CHART OR PICTURE, LISTING THE THEME OF YOUR APPEAL

PAGE 3 — MISSION STATEMENT

(Insert your mission statement here)

We accomplish our mission through our ministries of:
WORSHIP, LEARNING, SUPPORT, WITNESS, SERVICE
and through
OUR PARTNERSHIP in the _____ [denomination]

LOOK AT THE WAYS WE ARE NOW SERVING,
AND AT OUR VISION FOR
19__:

PAGE 4 (example)

WORSHIP

- Worship services at _____ A.M. every Sunday, with Holy Communion offered _____.
- Midweek services during Advent and Lent.
- Festival services at Christmas, Easter, Pentecost, and _____ Sunday and _____.
- Chapel always open for prayer.

★ ★ ★

MINISTRY OPPORTUNITIES FOR ALL MEMBERS

• CHOIR • USHERING • READING LESSONS •
• ALTAR GUILD • WORSHIP AND MUSIC COMMITTEE •

★ ★ ★

OUR VISION FOR MINISTRY IN 19__ WOULD
STRENGTHEN OUR MINISTRY OF WORSHIP BY:

- Increasing attendance.
- Adding a Saturday evening service.
- Encouraging more lay participation.
- Adding a children's choir.

To continue this worship ministry in 19__ will cost

$_____.

PAGE 5

SERVICE

- _____'s food shelf.
- Transportation for older members.
- Active social ministry committee.

★ ★ ★

MINISTRY OPPORTUNITIES FOR ALL MEMBERS:

• VOLUNTEER DRIVER • STUDY GROUPS •
• SOCIAL MINISTRY COMMITTEE •

★ ★ ★

OUR VISION FOR 19__ WOULD STRENGTHEN OUR
MINISTRY OF SERVICE BY:

- Regular visitation of the homebound and members in nursing centers.
- Special Purpose giving to provide medical assistance in _____.

To continue this ministry in 19__ will cost $_____.

PAGE 6

SUPPORT

- Dedicated staff (pastor, choir director, organist, secretary, etc. [use names]).
- Church governing body and committees administer the concerns of our congregation.
- Building and grounds used by the community, as well as by the congregation.

To continue this ministry of support in 19___ will cost
$_____.

★ ★ ★

MINISTRY OPPORTUNITIES FOR ALL MEMBERS:
• FINANCE COMMITTEE • PROPERTY COMMITTEE •
STEWARDSHIP COMMITTEE •
INDIVIDUALLY GIVING OF OUR
TIME, TALENTS, AND FINANCIAL SUPPORT

★ ★ ★

OUR VISION FOR 19___ WOULD STRENGTHEN OUR
MINISTRY OF SUPPORT BY:

• Increased emphasis on year-round stewardship.

• More effective use of time and abilities.

• Initiating a system of performance evaluation and merit-pay increases for our staff.

$_____ to show we care!

PAGE 7

WITNESS

• An active and growing evangelism committee:

• Participation in ecumenical activities.

• Ministerial association.

• Combined services.

• Advertising and publicity.

• Planned program of press releases.

• Posters in stores and community building.

• Paid newspaper ads on Sports and Living pages.

To continue this ministry in 19__ will cost $_____.

★ ★ ★

MINISTRY OPPORTUNITIES FOR ALL MEMBERS:

• DIALOGUES • CONGREGATIONAL VISITING •
• EVANGELISM COMMITTEE •

★ ★ ★

OUR VISION FOR 19__ WOULD STRENGTHEN OUR MINISTRY OF WITNESS BY:

• Calling on our inactive members.
• Establishing a greeter program to welcome everyone to worship.
• Televising Sunday services on cable TV.
$_____ to show we care!

PAGE 8

LEARNING

• Sunday school from three-year-old through adult
• Confirmation classes
• Wednesday morning Bible studies
• Vacation Bible School
• Library
• Youth camp
• Church Women
• Bible study, etc.

★ ★ ★

MINISTRY OPPORTUNITIES FOR ALL MEMBERS:

• SUNDAY SCHOOL TEACHERS AND ASSISTANTS •
• YOUTH GROUP SPONSORS •
• LIBRARY HELPERS — VBS TEACHERS AND HELPERS•
• CHRISTIAN EDUCATION COMMITTEE•

★ ★ ★

OUR VISION FOR 19__ WOULD STRENGTHEN OUR MINISTRY OF LEARNING BY:

• Opening our library on weekdays.

• Expanding our youth program.

• Camperships for young people.

To continue this ministry in 19__ will cost $_____.

PAGE 9

PARTNERSHIP

TOGETHER WITH THE REST OF THE _____ [denomination] WE:

• Teach pastors and professional church workers through SEMINARIES.

• Provide a solid Christian base for higher education through UNIVERSITIES.

• Serve persons in distress through SOCIAL SERVICES.

• Care for older people in _____ NURSING CENTERS.

• Provide Christian camping through _____.

• Serve God in harmony with other denominations through _____.

TOGETHER WITH MORE THAN _____ CONGREGA-
TIONS OF THE ___ [denomination] WE REACH OUT:

- Through special offerings for World Hunger.
- By setting our regular benevolence contributions through
  our church at ___% of our total income.
    To continue this ministry in 19__ will cost $_____.

PAGE 10

YES, WE ARE GOD'S PEOPLE, SENT TO SERVE . . .
AND YES, WE DO SERVE . . .
BUT GOD CALLS US TO DO EVEN MORE . . .
AND WE CAN DO MORE . . .

The Vision for Ministry presented in this brochure is our
challenge to do more.

To meet this challenge, it will take the participation of all
our members: our prayers, our time and abilities, and our
financial participation.

—We ask you to pray regularly and frequently for the
  ministries of _____ Church.
—We ask all of you to take advantage of the ministry
  opportunities that are offered, and to give of your time
  and abilities to see that all of them are accomplished.
  Just think what we could do if all _____ of us gave
  just one more hour a month to our congregation's ministries!
—We ask all of you to prayerfully consider increasing
  your estimate of giving. If all of us were to increase our
  giving by just one percent of our income, that would
  mean an additional $_____ for ministry! We could
  accomplish all of this Vision for Ministry . . . and MORE!

AS GOD'S PEOPLE, WE HAVE BEEN SENT TO DO
MINISTRY—TOGETHER, LET US SERVE!

APPENDIX D

PREPARING A TALLY OF APPEAL RESULTS

Explanation of worksheet:

1. Approximately ten days before the appeal, the financial secretary should prepare the preliminary data necessary on the sheet below. Congregations that pledge to both current expenses and benevolences will need to run a second set of sheets.
2. First, fill in the family names in alphabetical order in column 1. Be sure to include families that may have given nothing in the past; some will become new givers each year. Next, complete columns 2 and 3, using actual giving records (not pledges) for the past twelve months. *It is important to use the information for the last twelve months, rather than simply going back to last year's giving records. This system will be more up to date. It is also important that the figures used reflect the actual giving to ongoing ministry concerns of the congregation, and that it* **exclude special pass-through receipts** *(i.e., World Hunger offerings, a special one-time gift for a special cause, etc.).*
3. When commitments are returned, the financial secretary and assistants (persons privy to confidential records) should record column 4—members' pledges/estimates of giving per week for the next twelve months. After

recording all incoming estimates of giving, go back through the list to those lines with no figure in column 4. *Only* for those who have a blank line in column 4, place in column 5 the figure found in column 3.

4. Total columns 4 and 5 separately, then add them together.

5. Subtract the total of column 3 from the combined total of columns 4 and 5.

6. Divide the difference by the total of column 3 to find the percentage of increase anticipated in the coming year.

7. Compile a final report: Include percentage increase, new money to be received, income for last year, and income for the coming year. Report to the congregation.

FINAL CALCULATIONS WORKSHEET

Name (last name first)	Giving last 12 months	Giving last 12 months per week. (Column 2 ÷ 52 = ___)	Estimate of giving returned through appeal (per week)	Estimate based on last year's giving (col. 3) for those who did not estimate.
Totals				

APPENDIX E

QUESTIONS FOR
AN ENDOWMENT/TRUST FUND

1. *Should our congregation establish an endowment fund to receive gifts and bequests?* Yes, an endowment/trust fund can be God-pleasing for several reasons:

   A. Its purpose is the advancement of the mission of the church: "Go therefore and make disciples of all nations, baptizing them in the name of the Father and of the Son and of the Holy Spirit, and teaching them to obey everything that I have commanded you" (Matt. 28:19-20*a*).

   B. It reminds God's people that wills and estate planning are part of Christian stewardship, and as such are opportunities to put love into action for the family of God.

   C. It provides an orderly, established, and convenient means to receive and administer gifts and bequests for the benefit of Christ's mission.

2. *Should the endowment fund be a corporation separate from the congregation?* Except under unusual circumstances, it is neither advisable nor necessary to incorporate the endowment fund. The fund can be managed within the corporate structure of the congregation. For a more detailed explana-

148

tion, check with your denomination and an attorney for specific state regulations.

3. *Should the endowment fund be used to support the operating budget of the congregation?* The universal experience of congregations and church bodies says, "No!" There are two basic reasons: First, the common experience has been that this practice causes the members' financial support of the congregation to decline—so that the regular giving ends up supporting only that portion of the budget not covered by the endowment fund. Second, such a practice discourages members from making gifts and bequests to endowment funds.

It is better *not* to use the endowment for the operational budget, except under limited and catastrophic circumstances. Such a practice encourages members to continue to support the ministry of the congregation by tithing, first-fruits, and percentage giving, and also encourages them to support the extended ministries of the congregation by deferred giving to or through an endowment program.

4. *Should only the income be spent, or should both income and principal be available?* Authorities differ, but most suggest that the principal be available for distribution only in times of emergency. By building into the endowment document a means by which the principal may be used, the congregation allows for flexibility while not devastating the regular stewardship of members—some of whom might limit their giving until the principal is gone.

5. *Who should administer the endowment funds?* Following the advice of legal counsel, and in keeping with the organization of most congregations, experts generally suggest that the by-laws give authority to the church governing board to administer the fund. The governing board may, however, appoint advisory members who have the needed

expertise and experience to administer the fund. In addition, the congregation may use a foundation or trust officer for the financial management, leaving the governing board to concentrate on receipts of gifts and distribution of income.

NOTES

I. Foundations for Outward-Bound Living

1. Story based on the stewardship ministry of Richard Hollinger while pastor of St. Paul Lutheran Church in Clearwater, Fla.
2. Charles Sigel, "Biblical Foundations for Stewardship." Lecture presented in Orlando, Fla., 1988.

III. The Tour Guide's Role

3. An actual letter written by Pastor Steve Schick of Archbold, Ohio, to a young seminarian.
4. In a study conducted by Pastor Edward Uthe of the Evangelical Lutheran Church among congregations whose giving was double the national average, the number-one reason listed by the congregational leadership was "strong pastoral leadership."
5. *Christianity Today* (April 1980), Gallup Poll findings.
6. Edward Uthe, *Who Gives the Most?* (Chicago: Evangelical Lutheran Church in America Commission for Financial Support, August 16, 1989).

IV. To Pledge or Not to Pledge

7. Edward Uthe, *Program, Pledging, Tithing, Attendance: Their Relative Impacts on Giving* (Chicago: Evangelical Lutheran Church in America Commission for Financial Support, July 18, 1990).
8. Edgar Trexler, "A Fair Balance . . . ," *The Lutheran* (September 4, 1991), p. 50.
9. Dietrich Bonhoeffer, *The Cost of Discipleship* (New York: Macmillan Publishing Co., 1959), pp. 47-48.

VI. The Need of the Giver

10. Herb Miller, *Consecration Sunday Stewardship Program* Audio-cassette (Lubbock, Tex.: Net Press, 1990).

11. Edward Uthe, *Issue Paper: Designated Benevolence* (Chicago: Evangelical Lutheran Church in America, July 29, 1991).

12. Walter Wangerin, Jr., *Ragman and Other Cries of Faith* (New York: Harper & Row, 1984).

13. Carolyn Mowchan, *The Dance of the Heart: A Parable About Giving*. Leaflet Ministry Series (Minneapolis: Augsburg-Fortress Press, 1989).

VII. Variety Leads to Vitality

14. One of the most effective programs of this nature is written by Herb Miller, Net Press, 5001 Ave N, Lubbock, TX 79412.

15. Try *CommPac: A Contemporary Commitment Plan for Christian Stewardship*, produced through the cooperative efforts of twelve Canadian and United States denominations (New York: National Council of Churches, Commission on Stewardship, 1980).

16. One excellent direct mail approach is available from Vergil Hensley, Inc., 6116 East 32nd St., Tulsa, OK.

17. *The Circuit Rider Commitment Program* is available through Cokesbury bookstores or the Cokesbury Service Center, 1-800-672-1789 or 615-749-6113.

18. *Pony Express* is available from Rev. Don English Stewardship Resources, Inc., P.O. Box 75205, Oklahoma City, OK 73147.

19. *Up and Running* is available from Cokesbury bookstores or the Cokesbury Service Center, 1-800-672-1789 or 615-749-6113.

Other campaigns—the Celebrate series—can be obtained from Discipleship Resources: P.O. Box 187, Nashville TN 37202; 615-340-7284.

Celebrate Giving: A Financial Commitment Campaign outlines a ten-week process for planning and developing work calendars, job descriptions, designs for worship, and "sermon starters," and includes sample letters and commitment cards. ($6.95 each; 10 or more, $5.95 each—ST073K)

Celebrate & Visit: An Every Member Visitation Program is distinct from other types of financial campaigns in training members to share the financial plans of the congregation. Its joyful focus is on ministry, not money. ($6.95 each; 10 or more copies, $5.95 each—ST076K)

X. Ask the Vital Question

20. The information in this table was provided by Ms. Marjorie Spangler, assistant vice-president with the Federal Home Loan Bank of Cincinnati, Ohio.

21. Special thanks to Pastor Vernon H. Holmes, Division for Congregational Ministries of the Evangelical Lutheran Church in America for developing this suggestion for saving interest.